ontents

73

PHILADELPHIA Cream Cheese Tips for the Perfect Cheesecake

For best quality and results, always use PHILADELPHIA Cream Cheese.

Preheating the oven—The baking time indicated in a recipe is based on using a preheated oven. Turn the oven on when you start to mix the cheesecake ingredients. This should allow enough time for the oven to heat to the correct temperature for when you are ready to place the cheesecake in the oven to bake. Unless otherwise indicated, always bake cheesecakes in the center of the middle oven rack.

Beating the batter—While adding ingredients, do not overbeat the cheesecake batter. Too much air beaten into the batter will result in a cheesecake that sinks in the center when cooled.

Baking cheesecakes—Overbaked cheesecakes tend to crack. Remove cheesecake from oven when center is almost set (i.e. center of cheesecake still wiggles when pan is gently shaken from side-to-side). Although the cheesecake appears underbaked, the residual heat in the cheesecake will be enough to finish baking the center. After chilling, the cheesecake will have a perfectly smooth consistency.

Cooling cheesecakes—Cool cheesecakes completely before refrigerating. Placing a warm cheesecake in the refrigerator will cause condensation to form on the cake, resulting in a soggy cheesecake.

Cutting cheesecakes—Cut cheesecakes when they are cold rather than warm. Use a sharp knife with a clean, thin blade. To make clean cuts, dip the knife in hot water after each cut and wipe the blade clean.

For all of your occasions, PHILLY MAKES A BETTER CHEESECAKE.

During tests of plain New York-style cheesecake made with PHILADELPHIA Cream Cheese versus store-brand versions, consumers rated PHILLY cheesecake as better tasting.

No-Bake Desserts

FANTASTIC, OVEN-FREE DELIGHTS

OREO no-bake cheesecake

PREP: 15 min. plus refrigerating | MAKES: 24 servings, 1 piece each.

▶ what you need!

1 pkg. (1 lb. 2 oz.) OREO Chocolate Sandwich Cookies, divided

¼ cup (½ stick) butter, melted

4 pkg. (8 oz. each) PHILADELPHIA Cream Cheese, softened

½ cup sugar

1 tsp. vanilla

1 tub (8 oz.) COOL WHIP Whipped Topping, thawed

▶ make it!

1. **LINE** 13×9-inch pan with foil, with ends of foil extending over sides of pan. Coarsely chop 15 of the cookies; set aside. Finely crush remaining cookies; mix with butter. Press firmly onto bottom of prepared pan. Refrigerate while preparing filling.

2. **BEAT** cream cheese, sugar and vanilla in large bowl with electric mixer on medium speed until well blended. Gently stir in whipped topping and chopped cookies. Spoon over crust; cover.

3. **REFRIGERATE** 4 hours or until firm. Store leftover cheesecake in refrigerator.

SUBSTITUTE:
Prepare as directed, using Golden OREO Cookies.

PHILADELPHIA "fruit smoothie" no-bake cheesecake

PREP: 15 min. plus refrigerating | MAKES: 16 servings.

▶ what you need!

2 cups HONEY MAID Graham Cracker Crumbs

6 Tbsp. butter, melted

3 Tbsp. sugar

4 pkg. (8 oz. each) PHILADELPHIA Neufchâtel Cheese, softened

¾ cup sugar

1 pkg. (12 oz.) frozen mixed berries (strawberries, raspberries, blueberries and blackberries), thawed, well drained

1 tub (8 oz.) COOL WHIP LITE Whipped Topping, thawed

▶ make it!

1. **LINE** 13×9-inch pan with foil, with ends of foil extending over sides. Mix crumbs, butter and 3 Tbsp. sugar; press onto bottom of pan. Refrigerate while preparing filling.

2. **BEAT** Neufchâtel and ¾ cup sugar with mixer until well blended. Add berries; beat on low speed just until blended. Whisk in COOL WHIP. Pour over crust.

3. **REFRIGERATE** 4 hours or until firm. Use foil handles to lift cheesecake from pan before cutting to serve.

SPECIAL EXTRA:
Garnish with fresh berries just before serving.

VARIATION:
Prepare as directed, substituting 3 cups mixed fresh berries for the pkg. of frozen berries and increasing the sugar mixed with the Neufchâtel mixture to 1 cup.

fluffy cheesecake

PREP: 15 min. plus refrigerating | MAKES: 8 servings.

▶ what you need!

1 pkg. (8 oz.) PHILADELPHIA Cream Cheese, softened

⅓ cup sugar

1 tub (8 oz.) COOL WHIP Whipped Topping, thawed

1 HONEY MAID Graham Pie Crust (6 oz.)

1 apple, cored, thinly sliced

▶ make it!

1. **BEAT** cream cheese and sugar in large bowl with wire whisk or electric mixer until well blended. Gently stir in whipped topping.

2. **SPOON** into crust.

3. **REFRIGERATE** 3 hours or until set. Top with apple slices just before serving.

FLUFFY CHEESECAKE SQUARES:
Omit pie crust. Mix 1 cup HONEY MAID Graham Cracker Crumbs, 2 Tbsp. sugar and ⅓ cup melted butter or margarine. Press onto bottom of foil-lined 8-inch square pan. Continue as directed. Makes 9 servings.

FLUFFY CHERRY CHEESECAKE:
Prepare and refrigerate as directed. Top with 1½ cups cherry pie filling just before serving.

rocky road
no-bake cheesecake

PREP: 15 min. plus refrigerating | MAKES: 10 servings.

▶ what you need!

3 squares BAKER'S Semi-Sweet Chocolate, divided

2 pkg. (8 oz. each) PHILADELPHIA Cream Cheese, softened

⅓ cup sugar

¼ cup milk

2 cups thawed COOL WHIP Whipped Topping

¾ cup JET-PUFFED Miniature Marshmallows

⅓ cup chopped PLANTERS COCKTAIL Peanuts

1 OREO Pie Crust (6 oz.)

▶ make it!

1. **MICROWAVE** 1 chocolate square as directed on package. Coarsely chop remaining chocolate squares.

2. **BEAT** cream cheese, sugar and milk with mixer until well blended. Add melted chocolate; mix well. Whisk in COOL WHIP until well blended. Stir in chopped chocolate, marshmallows and nuts. Pour into crust.

3. **REFRIGERATE** 4 hours or until set.

SPECIAL EXTRA:
Shave 1 additional chocolate square. Use to garnish dessert along with additional marshmallows.

lem'n berry cheesecake

PREP: 10 min. plus refrigerating | MAKES: 8 servings.

▶ what you need!

1 pkg. (8 oz.) PHILADELPHIA Cream Cheese, softened

¼ cup COUNTRY TIME Lemonade Flavor Drink Mix

2 Tbsp. sugar

½ cup milk

2 cups thawed COOL WHIP Whipped Topping

1 HONEY MAID Graham Pie Crust (6 oz.)

1 cup assorted fresh berries

▶ make it!

1. **BEAT** cream cheese, drink mix and sugar in large bowl until well blended. Gradually add milk, mixing until well blended. Gently stir in whipped topping.

2. **SPOON** into crust.

3. **REFRIGERATE** 1 hour or until ready to serve. Garnish with berries.

GREAT SUBSTITUTE:
Prepare as directed, using PHILADELPHIA Neufchâtel Cheese and COOL WHIP LITE Whipped Topping.

PHILADELPHIA peaches 'n cream no-bake cheesecake

PREP: 15 min. plus refrigerating | MAKES: 16 servings.

▶ what you need!

2 cups HONEY MAID Graham Cracker Crumbs

6 Tbsp. margarine, melted

1 cup sugar, divided

4 pkg. (8 oz. each) PHILADELPHIA Neufchâtel Cheese, softened

1 pkg. (3 oz.) JELL-O Peach Flavor Gelatin

2 fresh peaches, chopped

1 tub (8 oz.) COOL WHIP LITE Whipped Topping, thawed

▶ make it!

1. **MIX** graham crumbs, margarine and ¼ cup sugar; press onto bottom of 13×9-inch pan. Refrigerate while preparing filling.

2. **BEAT** Neufchâtel and remaining sugar with mixer until well blended. Add dry gelatin mix; mix well. Stir in peaches and COOL WHIP; spread onto bottom of crust.

3. **REFRIGERATE** 4 hours or until firm.

SUBSTITUTE:
Prepare using 1 drained 15-oz. can peaches.

PHILADELPHIA no-bake chocolate-cherry cheesecake

PREP: 10 min. plus refrigerating | **MAKES:** 10 servings.

▶ what you need!

2 pkg. (8 oz. each) PHILADELPHIA Cream Cheese, softened

1 pkg. (4 oz.) BAKER'S GERMAN'S Sweet Chocolate, melted, cooled

⅓ cup sugar

1 tub (8 oz.) COOL WHIP Whipped Topping, thawed

1 HONEY MAID Graham Pie Crust (6 oz.)

1 can (21 oz.) cherry pie filling

▶ make it!

1. **BEAT** cream cheese, chocolate and sugar in large bowl with electric mixer on medium speed until well blended. Gently stir in whipped topping.

2. **SPOON** into crust.

3. **REFRIGERATE** 3 hours or overnight. Top with pie filling just before serving. Store leftover cheesecake in refrigerator.

chocolate-berry no-bake cheesecake

PREP: 15 min. plus refrigerating | MAKES: 10 servings.

▶ what you need!

2 squares BAKER'S Semi-Sweet Chocolate

2 pkg. (8 oz. each) PHILADELPHIA Cream Cheese, softened

⅓ cup sugar

2 cups thawed COOL WHIP Chocolate Whipped Topping

1 OREO Pie Crust (6 oz.)

1½ cups quartered strawberries

▶ make it!

1. **MICROWAVE** chocolate in small microwaveable bowl on HIGH 1 min.; stir until chocolate is completely melted. Set aside.

2. **BEAT** cream cheese and sugar in large bowl with electric mixer on medium speed until well blended. Add chocolate; mix well. Gently stir in whipped topping. Spoon into crust.

3. **REFRIGERATE** 3 hours or until set. Top with strawberries just before serving. Store leftover cheesecake in refrigerator.

PHILADELPHIA blueberry no-bake cheesecake

PREP: 15 min. plus refrigerating | MAKES: 16 servings, 1 piece each.

▶ what you need!

2 cups HONEY MAID Graham Cracker Crumbs

6 Tbsp. margarine, melted

1 cup sugar, divided

4 pkg. (8 oz. each) PHILADELPHIA Neufchâtel Cheese, softened

½ cup blueberry preserves

Grated peel from 1 lemon

1 pkg. (16 oz.) frozen blueberries, thawed, drained

1 tub (8 oz.) COOL WHIP LITE Whipped Topping, thawed

▶ make it!

1. **MIX** graham crumbs, margarine and ¼ cup of the sugar; press firmly onto bottom of 13×9-inch pan. Refrigerate while preparing filling.

2. **BEAT** Neufchâtel cheese and remaining ¾ cup sugar in large bowl with electric mixer on medium speed until well blended. Add preserves and lemon peel, mix until blended. Stir in blueberries. Gently stir in whipped topping. Spoon over crust; cover.

3. **REFRIGERATE** 4 hours or until firm. Garnish as desired. Store leftovers in refrigerator.

HOW TO MAKE IT WITH FRESH BLUEBERRIES:
Place 2 cups blueberries in small bowl with 2 Tbsp. sugar; mash with fork. Add to Neufchâtel cheese mixture; continue as directed.

PHILADELPHIA
strawberry fields
no-bake cheesecake

PREP: 15 min. plus refrigerating | MAKES: 16 servings, 1 piece each.

▶ what you need!

2 cups HONEY MAID Graham Cracker Crumbs

6 Tbsp. margarine, melted

1 cup sugar, divided

4 pkg. (8 oz. each) PHILADELPHIA Neufchâtel Cheese, softened

½ cup strawberry preserves

1 pkg. (16 oz.) frozen strawberries, thawed, drained

1 tub (8 oz.) COOL WHIP LITE Whipped Topping, thawed

▶ make it!

1. **MIX** graham crumbs, margarine and ¼ cup of the sugar; press firmly onto bottom of 13×9-inch pan. Refrigerate while preparing filling.

2. **BEAT** Neufchâtel cheese and remaining ¾ cup sugar in large bowl with electric mixer on medium speed until well blended. Add preserves; mix until blended. Stir in strawberries. Gently stir in whipped topping. Spoon over crust; cover.

3. **REFRIGERATE** 4 hours or until firm. Store leftovers in refrigerator.

HOW TO MAKE IT WITH FRESH STRAWBERRIES:
Place 2 cups fresh strawberries in small bowl with additional 2 Tbsp. sugar; mash with fork. Add to Neufchâtel cheese mixture; continue as directed.

PHILADELPHIA
chocolate cheesecakes
for two

PREP: 10 min. plus refrigerating | MAKES: 2 servings.

▶ what you need!

2 oz. (¼ of 8-oz. pkg.) PHILADELPHIA Cream Cheese, softened

1 Tbsp. sugar

1 square BAKER'S Semi-Sweet Chocolate, melted

½ cup thawed COOL WHIP Whipped Topping

2 OREO Chocolate Sandwich Cookies

▶ make it!

1. **BEAT** cream cheese, sugar and chocolate in medium bowl with wire whisk until well blended. Add whipped topping; mix well.

2. **PLACE** 1 cookie on bottom of each of 2 paper-lined medium muffin cups; fill evenly with cream cheese mixture.

3. **REFRIGERATE** 2 hours or overnight. (Or, if you are in a hurry, place in the freezer for 1 hour.)

PHILADELPHIA no-bake mini cheesecakes

PREP: 10 min. | MAKES: 12 servings.

▸ what you need!

1 pkg. (8 oz.) PHILADELPHIA Cream Cheese, softened

½ cup sugar

1 tub (8 oz.) COOL WHIP Whipped Topping, thawed

12 OREO Chocolate Sandwich Cookies

Multi-colored sprinkles

▸ make it!

1. **BEAT** cream cheese and sugar until well blended. Gently stir in whipped topping.

2. **PLACE** cookies on bottom of 12 paper-lined muffin cups.

3. **SPOON** cream cheese mixture into muffin cups. Top with multi-colored sprinkles. Refrigerate until ready to serve.

SUBSTITUTE:
Substitute miniature chocolate chips for sprinkles.

raspberry-lemon pie

PREP: 15 min. plus refrigerating | MAKES: 8 servings.

▶ what you need!

1 pkg. (8 oz.) PHILADELPHIA Cream Cheese, softened

1 pkg. (3.4 oz.) JELL-O Lemon Flavor Instant Pudding

1 cup cold milk

2 tsp. lemon zest

2 cups thawed COOL WHIP Whipped Topping, divided

1 HONEY MAID Graham Pie Crust (6 oz.)

1 cup fresh raspberries

▶ make it!

1. **BEAT** cream cheese, dry pudding mix, milk and lemon zest in large bowl with wire whisk until well blended. Gently stir in 1 cup of the whipped topping.

2. **SPOON** into crust; top with remaining 1 cup whipped topping.

3. **REFRIGERATE** 4 hours or until firm. Top with raspberries just before serving. Store leftover pie in refrigerator.

Classic
Cheesecakes

TIME-TESTED FAMILY FAVORITES

PHILADELPHIA
classic cheesecake

PREP: 20 min. | TOTAL: 5 hr. 45 min. (incl. refrigerating) | MAKES: 16 servings.

▶ what you need!

1½ cups HONEY MAID Graham Cracker Crumbs

3 Tbsp. sugar

⅓ cup butter or margarine, melted

4 pkg. (8 oz. each) PHILADELPHIA Cream Cheese, softened

1 cup sugar

1 tsp. vanilla

4 eggs

▶ make it!

HEAT oven to 325°F.

1. **MIX** crumbs, 3 Tbsp. sugar and butter; press onto bottom of 9-inch springform pan.

2. **BEAT** cream cheese, 1 cup sugar and vanilla with mixer until well blended. Add eggs, 1 at a time, mixing on low speed after each just until blended. Pour over crust.

3. **BAKE** 55 min. or until center is almost set. Loosen cake from rim of pan; cool before removing rim. Refrigerate 4 hours.

pumpkin swirl cheesecake

PREP: 20 min. | TOTAL: 5 hr. 35 min. (incl. refrigerating) | MAKES: 16 servings.

▶ what you need!

25 NABISCO Ginger Snaps, finely crushed (about 1½ cups)

½ cup finely chopped PLANTERS Pecans

¼ cup (½ stick) butter, melted

4 pkg. (8 oz. each) PHILADELPHIA Cream Cheese, softened

1 cup sugar, divided

1 tsp. vanilla

4 eggs

1 cup canned pumpkin

1 tsp. ground cinnamon

¼ tsp. ground nutmeg

Dash ground cloves

▶ make it!

HEAT oven to 325°F.

1. **LINE** 13×9-inch pan with foil, with ends of foil extending over sides. Mix ginger snap crumbs, nuts and butter; press onto bottom of pan.

2. **BEAT** cream cheese, ¾ cup sugar and vanilla with mixer until well blended. Add eggs, 1 at a time, mixing on low speed after each just until blended. Remove 1½ cups batter; place in small bowl. Stir remaining sugar, pumpkin and spices into remaining batter. Spoon half the pumpkin batter over crust; top with spoonfuls of half the plain batter. Repeat layers; swirl gently with knife.

3. **BAKE** 45 min. or until center is almost set. Cool completely. Refrigerate 4 hours. Use foil handles to lift cheesecake from pan before cutting to serve.

PHILADELPHIA new york-style sour cream-topped cheesecake

PREP: 15 min. | TOTAL: 5 hr. 5 min. (incl. refrigerating) | MAKES: 16 servings.

▶ what you need!

1½ cups HONEY MAID Graham Cracker Crumbs

¼ cup (½ stick) butter, melted

1¼ cups sugar, divided

4 pkg. (8 oz. each) PHILADELPHIA Cream Cheese, softened

2 tsp. vanilla, divided

1 container (16 oz.) BREAKSTONE'S or KNUDSEN Sour Cream, divided

4 eggs

2 cups fresh strawberries, sliced

▶ make it!

HEAT oven to 325°F.

1. **LINE** 13×9-inch pan with foil, with ends of foil extending over sides. Mix crumbs, butter and 2 Tbsp. sugar; press onto bottom of pan.

2. **BEAT** cream cheese, 1 cup of the remaining sugar and 1 tsp. vanilla in large bowl with mixer until well blended. Add 1 cup sour cream; mix well. Add eggs, 1 at a time, beating on low speed after each just until blended. Pour over crust.

3. **BAKE** 40 min. or until center is almost set. Mix remaining sour cream, sugar and vanilla; carefully spread over cheesecake. Bake 10 min. Cool completely. Refrigerate 4 hours. Use foil handles to lift cheesecake from pan before cutting to serve; top with berries.

PHILLY brownie cheesecake

PREP: 10 min. | TOTAL: 6 hr. (incl. refrigerating) | MAKES: 16 servings.

▶ what you need!

1 pkg. (19 to 21 oz.) brownie mix (13×9-inch pan size)

4 pkg. (8 oz. each) PHILADELPHIA Cream Cheese, softened

1 cup sugar

1 tsp. vanilla

½ cup BREAKSTONE'S or KNUDSEN Sour Cream

3 eggs

2 squares BAKER'S Semi-Sweet Chocolate

▶ make it!

HEAT oven to 325°F.

1. **PREPARE** brownie batter as directed on package; pour into 13×9-inch pan sprayed with cooking spray. Bake 25 min. or until top is shiny and center is almost set.

2. **MEANWHILE,** beat cream cheese, sugar and vanilla in large bowl with mixer until well blended. Add sour cream; mix well. Add eggs, 1 at a time, mixing on low speed after each just until blended. Gently pour over brownie layer in pan. (Filling will come almost to top of pan.)

3. **BAKE** 40 min. or until center is almost set. Run knife or metal spatula around rim of pan to loosen sides; cool. Refrigerate 4 hours.

4. **MELT** chocolate squares as directed on package; drizzle over cheesecake. Refrigerate 15 min. or until chocolate is firm.

caramel-nut cheesecake

PREP: 20 min. | TOTAL: 5 hr. 25 min. (incl. refrigerating) | MAKES: 16 servings.

▶ what you need!

2 cups HONEY MAID Graham Cracker Crumbs

1 cup PLANTERS COCKTAIL Peanuts, chopped, divided

1¼ cups sugar, divided

6 Tbsp. butter or margarine, melted

4 pkg. (8 oz. each) PHILADELPHIA Cream Cheese, softened

2 tsp. vanilla

1 cup BREAKSTONE'S or KNUDSEN Sour Cream

4 eggs

¼ cup caramel ice cream topping

▶ make it!

HEAT oven to 350°F.

1. **LINE** 13×9-inch pan with foil, with ends of foil extending over sides. Mix crumbs, ½ cup nuts, ¼ cup sugar and butter; press onto bottom of pan. Bake 10 min.

2. **MEANWHILE,** beat cream cheese, remaining sugar and vanilla with mixer until well blended. Add sour cream; mix well. Add eggs, 1 at a time, beating after each just until blended. Pour over crust.

3. **BAKE** 35 min. or until center is almost set; cool completely. Refrigerate 4 hours. Top with remaining nuts and caramel topping. Use foil handles to lift cheesecake from pan before cutting to serve.

SPECIAL EXTRA:
Cut chilled cheesecake into 16 bars, then cut each diagonally in half. Stack 2 on each dessert plate to serve.

HOW TO AVOID CRACKED CHEESECAKES:
After adding the eggs, be careful not to overbeat the batter since this can cause the baked cheesecake to crack.

PHILADELPHIA chocolate-vanilla swirl cheesecake

PREP: 15 min. | **TOTAL:** 5 hr. 25 min. (incl. refrigerating) | **MAKES:** 16 servings.

▶ what you need!

20 OREO Cookies, crushed (about 2 cups)

3 Tbsp. butter, melted

4 pkg. (8 oz. each) PHILADELPHIA Cream Cheese, softened

1 cup sugar

1 tsp. vanilla

1 cup BREAKSTONE'S or KNUDSEN Sour Cream

4 eggs

6 squares BAKER'S Semi-Sweet Chocolate, melted, cooled

▶ make it!

HEAT oven to 325°F.

1. **LINE** 13×9-inch pan with foil, with ends of foil extending over sides. Mix cookie crumbs and butter; press onto bottom of pan. Bake 10 min.

2. **BEAT** cream cheese, sugar and vanilla in large bowl with mixer until well blended. Add sour cream; mix well. Add eggs, 1 at a time, mixing after each just until blended.

3. **RESERVE** 1 cup batter. Stir chocolate into remaining batter; pour over crust. Top with spoonfuls of reserved plain batter; swirl with knife.

4. **BAKE** 40 min. or until center is almost set. Cool. Refrigerate 4 hours. Use foil handles to lift cheesecake from pan before cutting to serve. Garnish with chocolate curls, if desired.

HOW TO MAKE CHOCOLATE CURLS:
Let additional square(s) of BAKER'S Semi-Sweet Chocolate come to room temperature. Carefully draw a vegetable peeler at an angle across the chocolate square to make curls.

PHILADELPHIA
double-chocolate cheesecake

PREP: 20 min. | TOTAL: 5 hr. 35 min. (incl. refrigerating) | MAKES: 16 servings.

▶ what you need!

24 OREO Cookies, crushed (about 2¼ cups)

¼ cup (½ stick) butter or margarine, melted

4 pkg. (8 oz. each) PHILADELPHIA Cream Cheese, softened

1 cup sugar

2 Tbsp. flour

1 tsp. vanilla

1 pkg. (8 squares) BAKER'S Semi-Sweet Chocolate, melted, slightly cooled

4 eggs

▶ make it!

HEAT oven to 325°F.

1. **LINE** 13×9-inch pan with foil, with ends of foil extending over sides. Mix crumbs and butter; press onto bottom of pan. Bake 10 min.

2. **BEAT** cream cheese, sugar, flour and vanilla with mixer until well blended. Add chocolate; mix well. Add eggs, 1 at a time, mixing on low speed after each just until blended. Pour over crust.

3. **BAKE** 45 min. or until center is almost set. Cool completely. Refrigerate 4 hours. Use foil handles to lift cheesecake from pan before cutting to serve.

ultimate turtle cheesecake

PREP: 30 min. | TOTAL: 6 hr. 10 min. (incl. refrigerating) | MAKES: 16 servings.

▶ what you need!

2 cups OREO Chocolate Cookie Crumbs

6 Tbsp. butter or margarine, melted

1 pkg. (14 oz.) KRAFT Caramels

½ cup milk

1 cup chopped PLANTERS Pecans

3 pkg. (8 oz. each) PHILADELPHIA Cream Cheese, softened

¾ cup sugar

1 Tbsp. vanilla

3 eggs

2 squares BAKER'S Semi-Sweet Chocolate

▶ make it!

HEAT oven to 325°F.

1. **MIX** crumbs and butter; press onto bottom and 2 inches up side of 9-inch springform pan.

2. **MICROWAVE** caramels and milk in small microwaveable bowl on HIGH 3 min. or until caramels are completely melted, stirring after each minute. Stir in nuts; pour half into crust. Refrigerate 10 min. Refrigerate remaining caramel mixture for later use.

3. **BEAT** cream cheese, sugar and vanilla with mixer until well blended. Add eggs, 1 at a time, mixing on low speed after each just until blended. Pour over caramel layer in crust.

4. **BAKE** 1 hour 5 min. to 1 hour 10 min. or until center is almost set. Run knife around rim of pan to loosen cake; cool before removing rim. Refrigerate 4 hours.

5. **MICROWAVE** reserved caramel mixture 1 min.; stir. Pour over cheesecake. Melt chocolate as directed on package; drizzle over cheesecake.

chocolate bliss cheesecake

PREP: 20 min. | **TOTAL:** 6 hr. (incl. refrigerating) | **MAKES:** 12 servings.

▶ what you need!

18 OREO Cookies, finely crushed (about 1¾ cups)

2 Tbsp. butter or margarine, melted

3 pkg. (8 oz. each) PHILADELPHIA Cream Cheese, softened

¾ cup sugar

1 tsp. vanilla

1 pkg. (8 squares) BAKER'S Semi-Sweet Chocolate, melted, cooled slightly

3 eggs

▶ make it!

HEAT oven to 325°F.

1.

MIX crumbs and butter; press onto bottom of 9-inch springform pan.

2.

BEAT cream cheese, sugar and vanilla with mixer until well blended. Add chocolate; mix well. Add eggs, 1 at a time, mixing on low speed after each just until blended. Pour over crust.

3.

BAKE 55 min. to 1 hour or until center is almost set. Run knife around rim of pan to loosen cake; cool before removing rim. Refrigerate 4 hours. Garnish with powdered sugar and fresh raspberries just before serving, if desired.

lemon pudding cheesecake

PREP: 15 min. | TOTAL: 6 hr. (incl. refrigerating) | MAKES: 16 servings.

▶ what you need!

40 NILLA Wafers, crushed (about 1½ cups)

¾ cup plus 1 Tbsp. sugar, divided

3 Tbsp. butter or margarine, melted

4 pkg. (8 oz. each) PHILADELPHIA Cream Cheese, softened

2 Tbsp. flour

2 Tbsp. milk

1 cup BREAKSTONE'S or KNUDSEN Sour Cream

2 pkg. (3.4 oz. each) JELL-O Lemon Flavor Instant Pudding

4 eggs

2 squares BAKER'S White Chocolate

1 cup thawed COOL WHIP Strawberry Whipped Topping

▶ make it!

HEAT oven to 325°F.

1. **MIX** wafer crumbs, 1 Tbsp. sugar and butter; press firmly onto bottom of 9-inch springform pan. Bake 10 min.

2. **BEAT** cream cheese, remaining sugar, flour and milk with mixer until well blended. Add sour cream; mix well. Blend in dry pudding mixes. Add eggs, 1 at a time, mixing on low speed after each just until blended.

3. **BAKE** 1 hour 5 min. to 1 hour 15 min. or until center is almost set. Run knife around rim of pan to loosen cake; cool before removing rim. Refrigerate 4 hours. Meanwhile, prepare chocolate curls from white chocolate. Top cheesecake with COOL WHIP and chocolate curls just before serving.

HOW TO MAKE CHOCOLATE CURLS:
Melt chocolate as directed on package. Spread with spatula into very thin layer on baking sheet. Refrigerate 10 min., or until firm but still pliable. To make curls, push a metal spatula firmly along the baking sheet, under the chocolate, so the chocolate curls as it is pushed. (If chocolate is too firm to curl, let stand a few minutes at room temperature; refrigerate again if it becomes too soft.) Use toothpick to carefully place chocolate curls on waxed paper-covered tray. Refrigerate 15 min. or until firm. Use toothpick to arrange curls on dessert.

cappuccino cheesecake

PREP: 25 min. | TOTAL: 6 hr. 5 min. (incl. refrigerating) | MAKES: 16 servings.

▶ what you need!

1½ cups finely chopped PLANTERS Walnuts

3 Tbsp. butter or margarine, melted

2 Tbsp. sugar

4 pkg. (8 oz. each) PHILADELPHIA Cream Cheese, softened

1 cup sugar

3 Tbsp. flour

4 eggs

1 cup BREAKSTONE'S or KNUDSEN Sour Cream

1 Tbsp. MAXWELL HOUSE Instant Coffee

¼ tsp. ground cinnamon

¼ cup boiling water

1½ cups thawed COOL WHIP Whipped Topping

▶ make it!

HEAT oven to 325°F.

1. **MIX** nuts, butter and 2 Tbsp. sugar; press onto bottom of 9-inch springform pan. Bake 10 min. Remove from oven; cool. Increase oven temperature to 450°F.

2. **BEAT** cream cheese, 1 cup sugar and flour with mixer until well blended. Add eggs, 1 at a time, mixing on low speed after each just until blended. Blend in sour cream.

3. **DISSOLVE** instant coffee with cinnamon in water; cool. Gradually add to cream cheese mixture, mixing until well blended. Pour over crust.

4. **BAKE** 10 min. Reduce oven temperature to 250°F. Bake an additional 1 hour or until center is almost set. Run knife around rim of pan to loosen cake; cool before removing rim. Refrigerate 4 hours. Top with dollops of COOL WHIP. Garnish with a sprinkle of additional cinnamon, if desired.

OREO chocolate cheesecake

PREP: 30 min. | TOTAL: 5 hr. 45 min. (incl. refrigerating) | MAKES: 14 servings.

▶ what you need!

38 OREO Cookies, divided

5 Tbsp. butter or margarine, melted

5 squares BAKER'S Semi-Sweet Chocolate, divided

1 pkg. (8 oz.) PHILADELPHIA Cream Cheese, softened

½ cup plus 2 Tbsp. sugar, divided

1½ cups BREAKSTONE'S or KNUDSEN Sour Cream, divided

1 tsp. vanilla

2 eggs

▶ make it!

HEAT oven to 325°F.

1. **CRUSH** 24 cookies; mix with butter. Press onto bottom of 9-inch springform pan. Stand remaining cookies around inside edge of pan, firmly pressing bottom edge of each cookie into crust.

2. **MELT** 4 chocolate squares as directed on package. Beat cream cheese and ½ cup sugar with mixer until well blended. Add ½ cup sour cream, vanilla and chocolate; mix well. Add eggs, 1 at a time, mixing on low speed after each just until blended. Pour over crust.

3. **BAKE** 35 to 40 min. or until center is almost set. Mix remaining sour cream and sugar; spread over cheesecake. Bake 5 min. Run knife around rim of pan to loosen cake; cool before removing rim.

4. **MELT** remaining chocolate square; drizzle over cheesecake. Refrigerate 4 hours.

SPECIAL EXTRA:
Garnish as desired.

PHILADELPHIA black forest cheesecake

PREP: 15 min. | TOTAL: 4 hr. 55 min. (incl. refrigerating) | MAKES: 16 servings.

▶ what you need!

20 OREO Chocolate Sandwich Cookies, crushed (about 2 cups)

3 Tbsp. butter, melted

4 pkg. (8 oz. each) PHILADELPHIA Cream Cheese, softened

1 cup sugar

1 tsp. vanilla

1 cup BREAKSTONE'S or KNUDSEN Sour Cream

6 squares BAKER'S Semi-Sweet Chocolate, melted

4 eggs

2 cups thawed COOL WHIP Whipped Topping

1 can (21 oz.) cherry pie filling

▶ make it!

HEAT oven to 325°F.

1. **LINE** 13×9-inch baking pan with foil, with ends of foil extending over sides of pan. Mix cookie crumbs and butter; press firmly onto bottom of prepared pan. Bake 10 min.

2. **BEAT** cream cheese, sugar and vanilla in large bowl with electric mixer on medium speed until well blended. Add sour cream and chocolate; mix well. Add eggs, 1 at a time, mixing on low speed after each addition just until blended. Pour over crust.

3. **BAKE** 40 min. or until center is almost set. Cool. Refrigerate at least 4 hours or overnight. Lift cheesecake from pan, using foil handles. Top with whipped topping and pie filling. Store any leftover cheesecake in refrigerator.

chocolate truffle cheesecake

PREP: 15 min. | TOTAL: 2 hr. 25 min. (incl. refrigerating) | MAKES: 16 servings.

▶ what you need!

18 OREO Chocolate Sandwich Cookies, finely crushed (about 1¾ cups)

2 Tbsp. butter or margarine, melted

3 pkg. (8 oz. each) PHILADELPHIA Cream Cheese, softened

1 can (14 oz.) sweetened condensed milk

2 tsp. vanilla

1 pkg. (12 oz.) BAKER'S Semi-Sweet Chocolate Chunks, melted, slightly cooled

4 eggs

▶ make it!

HEAT oven to 300°F.

1. **MIX** cookie crumbs and butter; press firmly onto bottom of 9-inch springform pan. Set aside.

2. **BEAT** cream cheese, sweetened condensed milk and vanilla in large bowl with electric mixer on medium speed until well blended. Add chocolate; mix well. Add eggs, 1 at a time, mixing on low speed after each addition just until blended. Pour over crust.

3. **BAKE** 1 hour 5 min. or until center is almost set. Run knife or metal spatula around rim of pan to loosen cake; cool before removing rim of pan. Refrigerate at least 4 hours or overnight. Garnish as desired. Store leftover cheesecake in refrigerator.

white chocolate cheesecake

PREP: 30 min. | TOTAL: 6 hr. 30 min. (incl. refrigerating) | MAKES: 16 servings.

▶ what you need!

¾ cup sugar, divided

½ cup (1 stick) butter, softened

1½ tsp. vanilla, divided

1 cup flour

4 pkg. (8 oz. each) PHILADELPHIA Cream Cheese, softened

2 pkg. (6 squares each) BAKER'S Premium White Chocolate, melted, slightly cooled

4 eggs

1 pt. (2 cups) fresh raspberries

▶ make it!

HEAT oven to 325°F.

1. **BEAT** ¼ cup of the sugar, the butter and ½ tsp. of the vanilla in small bowl with electric mixer on medium speed until light and fluffy. Gradually add flour, mixing on low speed until well blended after each addition. Press firmly onto bottom of 9-inch springform pan; prick with fork. Bake 25 min. or until edge is lightly browned.

2. **BEAT** cream cheese, remaining ½ cup sugar and remaining 1 tsp. vanilla in large bowl with electric mixer on medium speed until well blended. Add melted chocolate; mix well. Add eggs, 1 at a time, beating on low speed after each addition just until blended. Pour over crust.

3. **BAKE** 55 min. to 1 hour or until center is almost set. Run knife or metal spatula around rim of pan to loosen cake; cool before removing rim of pan. Refrigerate 4 hours or overnight. Top with the raspberries just before serving. Store leftover cheesecake in refrigerator.

SPECIAL EXTRA:
Garnish with finely chopped fresh mint just before serving.

PHILADELPHIA 3-STEP
coconut cheesecake

PREP: 10 min. | TOTAL: 4 hr. 50 min. (incl. refrigerating) | MAKES: 10 servings.

▶ what you need!

2 pkg. (8 oz. each) PHILADELPHIA Cream Cheese, softened

½ cup cream of coconut

½ cup sugar

½ tsp. vanilla

2 eggs

1 HONEY MAID Graham Pie Crust (6 oz.)

2 cups thawed COOL WHIP Whipped Topping

½ cup BAKER'S ANGEL FLAKE Coconut, toasted

▶ make it!

HEAT oven to 350°F.

1. **BEAT** cream cheese, cream of coconut, sugar and vanilla with electric mixer on medium speed until well blended. Add eggs; mix just until blended.

2. **POUR** into crust.

3. **BAKE** 40 min. or until center is almost set. Cool. Refrigerate 3 hours or overnight. Top with whipped topping and toasted coconut just before serving. Store leftover cheesecake in refrigerator.

PHILADELPHIA 3-STEP chocolate chip cheesecake

PREP: 10 min. | TOTAL: 4 hr. 50 min. (incl. refrigerating) | MAKES: 8 servings.

▶ what you need!

2 pkg. (8 oz. each) PHILADELPHIA Cream Cheese, softened

½ cup sugar

½ tsp. vanilla

2 eggs

¾ cup miniature semi-sweet chocolate chips, divided

1 HONEY MAID Graham Pie Crust (6 oz.)

▶ make it!

HEAT oven to 350°F.

1. **BEAT** cream cheese, sugar and vanilla in large bowl with electric mixer on medium speed until well blended. Add eggs; mix just until blended. Stir in ½ cup of the chips.

2. **POUR** into crust. Sprinkle with remaining ¼ cup chips.

3. **BAKE** 40 min. or until center is almost set. Cool. Refrigerate 3 hours or overnight. Store leftover cheesecake in refrigerator.

PHILADELPHIA 3-STEP toffee crunch cheesecake

PREP: 10 min. | TOTAL: 4 hr. 50 min. (incl. refrigerating) | MAKES: 8 servings.

▶ what you need!

2 pkg. (8 oz. each) PHILADELPHIA Cream Cheese, softened

½ cup firmly packed brown sugar

½ tsp. vanilla

2 eggs

4 chocolate-covered English toffee bars (1.4 oz. each), chopped (about 1 cup), divided

1 HONEY MAID Graham Pie Crust (6 oz.)

▶ make it!

HEAT oven to 350°F.

1. **BEAT** cream cheese, sugar and vanilla in large bowl with electric mixer on medium speed until well blended. Add eggs; mix just until blended. Stir in ¾ cup of the chopped toffee bars.

2. **POUR** into crust. Sprinkle with remaining chopped toffee bars.

3. **BAKE** 35 to 40 min. or until center is almost set. Cool. Refrigerate 3 hours or overnight. Store leftover cheesecake in refrigerator.

GREAT SUBSTITUTE:
For extra chocolate flavor, substitute 1 OREO Pie Crust (6 oz.) for the graham pie crust.

ribbon bar cheesecake

PREP: 15 min. | TOTAL: 5 hr. 15 min. (incl. refrigerating) | MAKES: 16 servings.

▶ what you need!

30 OREO Chocolate Sandwich Cookies, crushed (about 3 cups)

½ cup (1 stick) butter, melted

¼ cup chopped PLANTERS Pecans

¼ cup BAKER'S ANGEL FLAKE Coconut

4 pkg. (8 oz. each) PHILADELPHIA Cream Cheese, softened

1 cup sugar

4 eggs

½ cup whipping cream

6 squares BAKER'S Semi-Sweet Chocolate

▶ make it!

HEAT oven to 350°F.

1. **MIX** crushed cookies, butter, pecans and coconut; press firmly onto bottom of 13×9-inch baking pan. Refrigerate while preparing filling.

2. **BEAT** cream cheese and sugar in large bowl with electric mixer on medium speed until well blended. Add eggs, 1 at a time, mixing on low speed after each addition just until blended. Pour over crust.

3. **BAKE** 40 min. or until center is almost set. Cool. Refrigerate 3 hours or overnight. Place whipping cream and chocolate in saucepan. Cook on low heat until chocolate is completely melted and mixture is well blended, stirring occasionally. Pour over cheesecake. Refrigerate 15 min. or until chocolate is firm. Store leftover cheesecake in refrigerator.

JAZZ IT UP:
After chocolate topping is firm, place 1 additional chocolate square in microwaveable bowl. Microwave on MEDIUM 1 min., stirring after 30 sec. Stir until chocolate is completely melted. Pour into small resealable bag; seal bag. Snip off one small corner from bottom of bag; twist top of bag to squeeze chocolate from bag to pipe a special message, such as "Greetings," on top of cheesecake.

double-layer pumpkin cheesecake

PREP: 10 min. | TOTAL: 4 hr. 20 min. (incl. refrigerating) | MAKES: 8 servings.

▶ what you need!

2 pkg. (8 oz. each) PHILADELPHIA Fat Free Cream Cheese, softened

½ cup sugar

½ tsp. vanilla

2 eggs

½ cup canned pumpkin

¼ tsp. ground cinnamon

Dash ground nutmeg

⅓ cup HONEY MAID Graham Cracker Crumbs

½ cup thawed COOL WHIP Sugar Free Whipped Topping

▶ make it!

HEAT oven to 325°F.

1. **BEAT** cream cheese, sugar and vanilla with mixer until well blended. Beat in eggs, 1 at a time, just until blended. Remove 1 cup batter; place in medium bowl. Stir in pumpkin and spices.

2. **SPRAY** 9-inch pie plate with cooking spray; sprinkle bottom and side with crumbs.

3. **TOP** with layers of plain and pumpkin batters. Bake 40 min. or until center is almost set. Cool completely. Refrigerate 3 hours. Serve topped with COOL WHIP.

SPECIAL EXTRA:
Garnish with additional cinnamon.

chocolate chunk cheesecake

PREP: 10 min. | TOTAL: 4 hr. 45 min. (incl. refrigerating) | MAKES: 16 servings.

▶ what you need!

18 OREO Cookies, crushed (about 1¾ cups)

¼ cup (½ stick) butter, melted

3 pkg. (8 oz. each) PHILADELPHIA Cream Cheese, softened

¾ cup sugar

½ cup BREAKSTONE'S or KNUDSEN Sour Cream

3 eggs

1½ pkg. (8 squares each) BAKER'S Semi-Sweet Chocolate, divided

½ cup whipping cream

▶ make it!

HEAT oven to 350°F.

1. **MIX** crumbs and butter; press onto bottom of 9-inch springform pan.

2. **BEAT** cream cheese and sugar in large bowl with mixer until well blended. Add sour cream; mix well. Add eggs, 1 at a time, beating on low speed after each just until blended. Chop 8 chocolate squares; stir into batter. Pour over crust.

3. **BAKE** 45 to 50 min. or until center is almost set. Run knife around rim of pan to loosen cake. Cool completely.

4. **BRING** cream to simmer in small saucepan on low heat. Meanwhile, chop remaining chocolate squares. Remove pan from heat. Add chocolate; stir until completely melted. Cool slightly. Pour over cheesecake. Refrigerate 3 hours. Remove rim of pan before serving cheesecake.

HOW TO SOFTEN CREAM CHEESE:
Place completely unwrapped pkg. of cream cheese in microwaveable bowl. Microwave on HIGH 30 sec. or until slightly softened.

Fruity Favorites

CHEESECAKES PAIRED WITH FRUIT FLAVORS

lemon cheesecake

PREP: 15 min. | TOTAL: 6 hr. 5 min. (incl. refrigerating) | MAKES: 12 servings.

▶ what you need!

1½ cups HONEY MAID Graham Cracker Crumbs

1¼ cups sugar, divided

3 Tbsp. butter or margarine, melted

3 pkg. (8 oz. each) PHILADELPHIA Cream Cheese, softened

1 cup BREAKSTONE'S or KNUDSEN Sour Cream

Grated peel and juice from 1 medium lemon

3 eggs

▶ make it!

HEAT oven to 350°F.

1. **MIX** crumbs, ¼ cup of the sugar and butter. Reserve ½ cup of the crumb mixture; press remaining crumb mixture firmly onto bottom of 9-inch springform pan. Set aside.

2. **BEAT** cream cheese and remaining 1 cup sugar in large bowl with electric mixer on medium speed until well blended. Add sour cream, lemon peel and juice; mix well. Add eggs, 1 at a time, beating on low speed after each addition just until blended. Pour over crust; sprinkle with reserved crumb mixture.

3. **BAKE** 45 to 50 min. or until center is almost set. Turn off oven. Open door slightly; let cheesecake stand in oven 30 min. Remove to wire rack. Run knife or metal spatula around rim of pan to loosen cake; cool before removing rim of pan. Refrigerate at least 4 hours or overnight. Garnish as desired. Store leftover cheesecake in refrigerator.

HOW TO SOFTEN CREAM CHEESE:
Place completely unwrapped pkg. of cream cheese on microwaveable plate. Microwave on HIGH 15 to 20 sec. or until slightly softened.

PHILADELPHIA
new york-style strawberry swirl cheesecake

PREP: 15 min. | TOTAL: 5 hr. 25 min. (incl. refrigerating) | MAKES: 16 servings.

▶ what you need!

1 cup HONEY MAID Graham Cracker Crumbs

3 Tbsp. sugar

3 Tbsp. butter, melted

5 pkg. (8 oz. each) PHILADELPHIA Cream Cheese, softened

1 cup sugar

3 Tbsp. flour

1 Tbsp. vanilla

1 cup BREAKSTONE'S or KNUDSEN Sour Cream

4 eggs

⅓ cup seedless strawberry jam

▶ make it!

HEAT oven to 325°F.

1. **LINE** 13×9-inch pan with foil, with ends of foil extending over sides. Mix cracker crumbs, 3 Tbsp. sugar and butter; press onto bottom of pan. Bake 10 min.

2. **BEAT** cream cheese, 1 cup sugar, flour and vanilla in large bowl with mixer until well blended. Add sour cream; mix well. Add eggs, 1 at a time, mixing on low speed after each just until blended. Pour over crust. Gently drop small spoonfuls of jam over batter; swirl with knife.

3. **BAKE** 40 min. or until center is almost set. Cool completely. Refrigerate 4 hours. Use foil handles to lift cheesecake from pan before cutting to serve.

PHILADELPHIA
new york cheesecake

PREP: 15 min. | TOTAL: 5 hr. 25 min. (incl. refrigerating) | MAKES: 16 servings.

▶ what you need!

20 OREO Cookies, finely crushed (about 2 cups)

3 Tbsp. butter or margarine, melted

5 pkg. (8 oz. each) PHILADELPHIA Cream Cheese, softened

1 cup sugar

3 Tbsp. flour

1 Tbsp. vanilla

1 cup BREAKSTONE'S or KNUDSEN Sour Cream

4 eggs

1 can (21 oz.) cherry pie filling

▶ make it!

HEAT oven to 325°F.

1.

LINE 13×9-inch pan with foil, with ends of foil extending over sides. Mix crumbs and butter; press onto bottom of pan.

2.

BEAT cream cheese, sugar, flour and vanilla with mixer until well blended. Add sour cream; mix well. Add eggs, 1 at a time, mixing on low speed after each just until blended. Pour over crust.

3.

BAKE 40 min. or until center is almost set. Cool completely. Refrigerate 4 hours. Use foil handles to lift cheesecake from pan before cutting to serve. Top with pie filling.

scrumptious apple-pecan cheesecake

PREP: 25 min. | TOTAL: 6 hr. 10 min. (incl. refrigerating) | MAKES: 12 servings.

▶ what you need!

1 cup HONEY MAID Graham Cracker Crumbs

¾ cup finely chopped PLANTERS Pecans, divided

3 Tbsp. sugar

1 tsp. ground cinnamon, divided

¼ cup (½ stick) butter or margarine, melted

2 pkg. (8 oz. each) PHILADELPHIA Cream Cheese, softened

½ cup sugar

½ tsp. vanilla

2 eggs

⅓ cup sugar

4 cups thin peeled apple slices

▶ make it!

HEAT oven to 325°F.

1. **MIX** crumbs, ½ cup nuts, 3 Tbsp. sugar, ½ tsp. cinnamon and butter; press onto bottom of 9-inch springform pan. Bake 10 min.

2. **BEAT** cream cheese, ½ cup sugar and vanilla with mixer until well blended. Add eggs, 1 at a time, beating on low speed after each just until blended. Pour over crust. Mix ⅓ cup sugar and remaining cinnamon in large bowl. Add apples; toss to coat. Spoon over cream cheese layer; sprinkle with remaining nuts.

3. **BAKE** 1 hour 10 min. to 1 hour 15 min. or until center is almost set. Run knife around rim of pan to loosen cake; cool before removing rim. Refrigerate 4 hours.

PHILLY blueberry swirl cheesecake

PREP: 15 min. | TOTAL: 7 hr. (incl. refrigerating) | MAKES: 16 servings.

▶ what you need!

1 cup HONEY MAID Graham Cracker Crumbs

1 cup plus 3 Tbsp. sugar, divided

3 Tbsp. butter or margarine, melted

4 pkg. (8 oz. each) PHILADELPHIA Cream Cheese, softened

1 tsp. vanilla

1 cup BREAKSTONE'S or KNUDSEN Sour Cream

4 eggs

2 cups fresh or thawed frozen blueberries

▶ make it!

HEAT oven to 325°F.

1. **MIX** crumbs, 3 Tbsp. of the sugar and the butter. Press firmly onto bottom of foil-lined 13×9-inch baking pan. Bake 10 min.

2. **BEAT** cream cheese, remaining 1 cup sugar and the vanilla in large bowl with electric mixer on medium speed until well blended. Add sour cream; mix well. Add eggs, 1 at a time, beating on low speed after each addition just until blended. Pour over crust. Purée the blueberries in a blender or food processor. Gently drop spoonfuls of the puréed blueberries over batter; cut through batter several times with knife for marble effect.

3. **BAKE** 45 min. or until center is almost set; cool. Refrigerate at least 4 hours or overnight. Garnish as desired. Store leftover cheesecake in refrigerator.

our best chocolate cheesecake

PREP: 30 min. | TOTAL: 5 hr. 35 min. (incl. refrigerating) | MAKES: 16 servings.

▶ what you need!

18 OREO Chocolate Sandwich Cookies, crushed (about 1¾ cups)

2 Tbsp. butter or margarine, melted

3 pkg. (8 oz. each) PHILADELPHIA Cream Cheese, softened

1 cup sugar

1 tsp. vanilla

1 pkg. (8 squares) BAKER'S Semi-Sweet Chocolate, melted, slightly cooled

3 eggs

1 cup thawed COOL WHIP DIPS Strawberry Crème

1½ cups assorted seasonal fruit, such as chopped strawberries and sliced kiwi

▶ make it!

HEAT oven to 325°F.

1. **MIX** crushed cookies and butter; press firmly onto bottom of 9-inch springform pan. Bake 10 min.

2. **BEAT** cream cheese, sugar and vanilla with electric mixer on medium speed until well blended. Add chocolate; mix well. Add eggs, 1 at a time, mixing on low speed after each addition just until blended. Pour over crust.

3. **BAKE** 45 to 55 min. or until center is almost set. Run knife or metal spatula around rim of pan to loosen cake; cool before removing rim of pan. Refrigerate 4 hours or overnight. Top with COOL WHIP DIPS and fruit.

HOW TO SOFTEN CREAM CHEESE:
Place completely unwrapped pkg. of cream cheese in microwaveable bowl.
Microwave on HIGH 45 sec. or until slightly softened.

VARIATION:
This recipe can also be made in a greased, foil-lined 13×9-inch baking pan.
Reduce the baking time by 5 to 10 min.

triple-citrus cheesecake

PREP: 30 min. | TOTAL: 6 hr. 35 min. (incl. refrigerating) | MAKES: 16 servings.

▶ what you need!

1 cup HONEY MAID Graham Cracker Crumbs

⅓ cup firmly packed brown sugar

¼ cup (½ stick) butter or margarine, melted

4 pkg. (8 oz. each) PHILADELPHIA Cream Cheese, softened

1 cup granulated sugar

2 Tbsp. flour

1 tsp. vanilla

4 eggs

1 Tbsp. fresh lemon juice

1 Tbsp. fresh lime juice

1 Tbsp. fresh orange juice

1 tsp. grated lemon peel

1 tsp. grated lime peel

1 tsp. grated orange peel

▶ make it!

HEAT oven to 325°F.

1. **MIX** crumbs, brown sugar and butter; press firmly onto bottom of 9-inch springform pan. Bake 10 min.

2. **BEAT** cream cheese, granulated sugar, flour and vanilla with electric mixer on medium speed until well blended. Add eggs, 1 at a time, mixing on low speed after each addition just until blended. Stir in remaining ingredients; pour over crust.

3. **BAKE** 1 hour 5 min. or until center is almost set. Run knife or metal spatula around rim of pan to loosen cake; cool before removing rim of pan. Refrigerate 4 hours or overnight. Garnish as desired. Store leftover cheesecake in refrigerator.

PHILADELPHIA 3-STEP
key lime cheesecake

PREP: 10 min. | TOTAL: 3 hr. 10 min. (incl. refrigerating) | MAKES: 8 servings.

▶ what you need!

2 pkg. (8 oz. each) PHILADELPHIA Cream Cheese, softened

½ cup sugar

1 tsp. lime zest

2 Tbsp. lime juice

½ tsp. vanilla

2 eggs

1 HONEY MAID Graham Pie Crust (6 oz.)

1 cup thawed COOL WHIP Whipped Topping

▶ make it!

HEAT oven to 350°F.

1. **BEAT** first 5 ingredients with mixer until well blended. Add eggs; mix just until blended.

2. **POUR** into crust.

3. **BAKE** 40 min. or until center is almost set. Cool. Refrigerate 3 hours. Top with COOL WHIP just before serving.

SPECIAL EXTRA:
Garnish with lime slices just before serving.

white chocolate-cherry pecan cheesecake

PREP: 30 min. | TOTAL: 6 hr. 30 min. (incl. refrigerating) | MAKES: 16 servings.

▶ what you need!

1 cup PLANTERS Pecan Halves, toasted, divided

1½ cups HONEY MAID Graham Cracker Crumbs

¼ cup sugar

¼ cup (½ stick) margarine or butter, melted

3 pkg. (8 oz. each) PHILADELPHIA Cream Cheese, softened

1 can (14 oz.) sweetened condensed milk

1 pkg. (6 squares) BAKER'S Premium White Chocolate, melted

2 tsp. vanilla, divided

4 eggs

1 can (21 oz.) cherry pie filling

1 cup thawed COOL WHIP Whipped Topping

▶ make it!

HEAT oven to 300°F.

1. **RESERVE** 16 of the pecan halves for garnish. Finely chop remaining pecans; mix with graham crumbs, sugar and margarine. Press firmly onto bottom of 9-inch springform pan.

2. **BEAT** cream cheese in large bowl with electric mixer on medium speed until creamy. Gradually add sweetened condensed milk, beating until well blended. Add chocolate and 1 tsp. of the vanilla; mix well. Add eggs, 1 at a time, mixing on low speed after each addition just until blended. Pour over crust.

3. **BAKE** 1 hour or until center is almost set. Run knife or metal spatula around rim of pan to loosen cake; cool before removing rim of pan. Refrigerate 4 hours or overnight.

4. **MIX** pie filling and remaining 1 tsp. vanilla; spoon over cheesecake. Top with whipped topping and reserved pecans. Cut into wedges to serve. Store leftover cheesecake in refrigerator.

PHILADELPHIA 3-STEP amaretto-berry cheesecake

PREP: 10 min. | TOTAL: 5 hr. 50 min. (incl. refrigerating) | MAKES: 8 servings.

▶ what you need!

2 pkg. (8 oz. each) PHILADELPHIA Cream Cheese, softened

½ cup sugar

½ tsp. vanilla

3 Tbsp. almond-flavored liqueur

2 eggs

1 HONEY MAID Graham Pie Crust (6 oz.)

2 cups mixed berries (blueberries, raspberries, sliced strawberries)

▶ make it!

HEAT oven to 350°F.

1. **BEAT** cream cheese, sugar and vanilla in large bowl with electric mixer on medium speed until well blended. Add liqueur; mix well. Add eggs; beat just until blended.

2. **POUR** into crust.

3. **BAKE** 35 to 40 min. or until center is almost set. Cool. Refrigerate 3 hours or overnight. Top with berries just before serving. Store leftover cheesecake in refrigerator.

HOW TO SOFTEN CREAM CHEESE:
Place completely unwrapped pkg. of cream cheese on microwaveable plate. Microwave on HIGH 20 sec. or until slightly softened.

GREAT SUBSTITUTE:
Substitute 1 tsp. almond extract for the almond-flavored liqueur.

PHILADELPHIA 3-STEP
white chocolate-raspberry swirl cheesecake

PREP: 10 min. | TOTAL: 5 hr. 50 min. (incl. refrigerating) | MAKES: 8 servings.

▶ what you need!

2 pkg. (8 oz. each) PHILADELPHIA Cream Cheese, softened

½ cup sugar

½ tsp. vanilla

2 eggs

3 squares BAKER'S Premium White Chocolate, melted

1 OREO Pie Crust (6 oz.)

3 Tbsp. raspberry preserves

▶ make it!

HEAT oven to 350°F.

1. **BEAT** cream cheese, sugar and vanilla with electric mixer on medium speed until well blended. Add eggs; mix just until blended. Stir in white chocolate. Pour into crust.

2. **MICROWAVE** preserves in small bowl on HIGH 15 sec. or until melted. Dot top of cheesecake with small spoonfuls of preserves. Cut through batter with knife several times for marble effect.

3. **BAKE** 35 to 40 min. or until center is almost set. Cool. Refrigerate 3 hours or overnight. Store leftover cheesecake in refrigerator.

white chocolate-cranberry cheesecake

PREP: 15 min. | TOTAL: 5 hr. 5 min. (incl. refrigerating) | MAKES: 12 servings.

▶ what you need!

1¼ cups OREO Chocolate Cookie Crumbs

¼ cup (½ stick) butter, melted

3 pkg. (8 oz. each) PHILADELPHIA Cream Cheese, softened

¾ cup sugar

3 eggs

4 squares BAKER'S Premium White Chocolate, melted

½ cup dried cranberries

1 tsp. grated orange peel

▶ make it!

HEAT oven to 350°F.

1. **MIX** crumbs and butter. Press onto bottom of 9-inch springform pan.

2. **BEAT** cream cheese and sugar in large bowl with electric mixer on medium speed until well blended. Add eggs, 1 at a time, mixing just until blended after each addition. Stir in white chocolate, cranberries and orange peel; pour over crust.

3. **BAKE** 45 to 50 min. or until center is almost set. Cool completely. Refrigerate 3 hours or overnight.

SPECIAL EXTRA
Garnish with thawed COOL WHIP Whipped Topping, orange slices and additional dried cranberries just before serving.

fruity cheesecake

PREP: 30 min. | TOTAL: 5 hr. 30 min. (incl. refrigerating) | MAKES: 24 servings.

▶ what you need!

60 NILLA Wafers, crushed (about 2 cups)

5 Tbsp. butter or margarine, melted

3 Tbsp. sugar

4 pkg. (8 oz. each) PHILADELPHIA Cream Cheese, softened

1 cup sugar

2 Tbsp. flour

1 cup BREAKSTONE'S or KNUDSEN Sour Cream

4 eggs

1 pkg. (3.4 oz.) JELL-O Lemon Flavor Instant Pudding

2 cups thawed COOL WHIP Whipped Topping

1 cup each blueberries, sliced fresh strawberries and sliced peeled kiwis

▶ make it!

HEAT oven to 325°F.

1. **LINE** 13×9-inch pan with foil, with ends of foil extending over sides. Mix wafer crumbs, butter and 3 Tbsp. sugar; press onto bottom of pan. Bake 10 min.

2. **BEAT** cream cheese, 1 cup sugar and flour in large bowl with mixer until well blended. Add sour cream; mix well. Add eggs, 1 at a time, beating on low speed after each just until blended. Stir in dry pudding mix. Pour over crust.

3. **BAKE** 1 hour or until center of cheesecake is almost set. Cool completely. Refrigerate 4 hours. Use foil handles to lift cheesecake from pan. Remove cheesecake from foil to tray; spread with COOL WHIP. Top with fruit just before serving.

contents

100

Seasonal Favorites

**SENSATIONAL SWEETS TO
ENJOY YEAR ROUND**

berry-berry cake

PREP: 25 min. | TOTAL: 2 hr. (incl. cooling) | MAKES: 12 servings.

▶ what you need!

⅓ cup PHILADELPHIA ⅓ Less Fat than Cream Cheese

¾ cup sugar, divided

2 egg whites

2 tsp. lemon zest

1 cup plus 2 tsp. flour, divided

½ tsp. baking soda

⅓ cup BREAKSTONE'S FREE or KNUDSEN FREE Fat Free Sour Cream

3 cups mixed fresh blueberries and raspberries, divided

▶ make it!

HEAT oven to 350°F.

1. BEAT reduced-fat cream cheese and ½ cup sugar in large bowl with mixer until well blended. Add egg whites and zest; mix well. Mix 1 cup flour and baking soda. Add to cream cheese mixture alternately with sour cream, beating well after each addition. (Do not overmix.)

2. SPREAD onto bottom and 1 inch up side of 9-inch springform pan sprayed with cooking spray. Toss 2 cups berries with remaining sugar and flour; spoon over cream cheese mixture in bottom of pan to within ½ inch of edge.

3. BAKE 40 to 45 min. or until toothpick inserted in center comes out clean. Run knife around rim of pan to loosen cake; cool before removing rim. Top cake with remaining berries. Keep refrigerated.

creamy lemon squares

PREP: 25 min. | TOTAL: 3 hr. 23 min. (incl. refrigerating) | MAKES: 16 servings.

▶ what you need!

20 Reduced Fat NILLA Wafers, finely crushed (about ¾ cup)

½ cup flour

¼ cup packed brown sugar

¼ cup (½ stick) cold margarine

1 pkg. (8 oz.) PHILADELPHIA Neufchâtel Cheese, softened

1 cup granulated sugar

2 eggs

2 Tbsp. flour

1 Tbsp. lemon zest

¼ cup fresh lemon juice

¼ tsp. CALUMET Baking Powder

2 tsp. powdered sugar

▶ make it!

HEAT oven to 350°F.

1. **LINE** 8-inch square pan with foil, with ends of foil extending over sides. Mix wafer crumbs, ½ cup flour and brown sugar in medium bowl. Cut in margarine with pastry blender or 2 knives until mixture resembles coarse crumbs; press onto bottom of prepared pan. Bake 15 min.

2. **MEANWHILE,** beat Neufchâtel and granulated sugar with mixer until well blended. Add eggs and 2 Tbsp. flour; mix well. Blend in lemon zest, lemon juice and baking powder; pour over crust.

3. **BAKE** 25 to 28 min. or until center is set. Cool completely. Refrigerate 2 hours. Sprinkle with powdered sugar just before serving.

SPECIAL EXTRA:
Garnish with lemon peel.

luscious four-layer pumpkin cake

PREP: 20 min. | TOTAL: 1 hr. 50 min. (incl. cooling) | MAKES: 16 servings.

▸ what you need!

1 pkg. (2-layer size) yellow cake mix

1 can (15 oz.) pumpkin, divided

½ cup milk

⅓ cup oil

4 eggs

1½ tsp. pumpkin pie spice, divided

1 pkg. (8 oz.) PHILADELPHIA Cream Cheese, softened

1 cup powdered sugar

1 tub (8 oz.) COOL WHIP Whipped Topping, thawed

¼ cup caramel ice cream topping

¼ cup PLANTERS Pecan Halves

▸ make it!

HEAT oven to 350°F.

1. **BEAT** cake mix, 1 cup pumpkin, milk, oil, eggs and 1 tsp. spice in large bowl with mixer until well blended. Pour into 2 greased and floured 9-inch round pans.

2. **BAKE** 28 to 30 min. or until toothpick inserted in centers comes out clean. Cool in pans 10 min. Remove from pans to wire racks; cool completely. Beat cream cheese in small bowl with mixer until creamy. Add sugar, remaining pumpkin and spice; mix well. Gently stir in COOL WHIP.

3. **CUT** each cake layer horizontally in half with serrated knife; stack on serving plate, spreading cream cheese filling between layers. (Do not frost top layer.) Drizzle with caramel topping just before serving; sprinkle with nuts. Refrigerate leftovers.

holiday cheesecake presents

PREP: 10 min. | TOTAL: 4 hr. 10 min. (incl. refrigerating) | MAKES: 32 servings.

▸ what you need!

1½ cups HONEY MAID Graham Cracker Crumbs

⅓ cup butter, melted

3 Tbsp. sugar

3 pkg. (8 oz. each) PHILADELPHIA Cream Cheese, softened

¾ cup sugar

1 tsp. vanilla

3 eggs

Suggested decorations: decorating gels, colored sprinkles

▸ make it!

HEAT oven to 350°F.

1. **MIX** crumbs, butter and 3 Tbsp. sugar; press onto bottom of 13×9-inch pan.

2. **BEAT** cream cheese, ¾ cup sugar and vanilla with mixer until well blended. Add eggs; mix just until blended. Pour over crust.

3. **BAKE** 30 min. or until center is almost set. Cool. Refrigerate 3 hours. Cut into bars. Decorate with gels and sprinkles to resemble presents.

VARIATION:
Substitute 50 NILLA Wafers, crushed (about 1½ cups), and ¼ cup (½ stick) butter, melted, for the HONEY MAID Graham Cracker Crumbs and ⅓ cup butter, melted.

snowball cake

PREP: 15 min. | **TOTAL:** 2 hr. 20 min. (incl. cooling) | **MAKES:** 16 servings.

▶ what you need!

1 pkg. (2-layer size) devil's food cake mix

1 pkg. (8 oz.) PHILADELPHIA Cream Cheese, softened

1 egg

2 Tbsp. granulated sugar

1 pkg. (3.4 oz.) JELL-O Vanilla Flavor Instant Pudding

¼ cup powdered sugar

1 cup cold milk

1 tub (8 oz.) COOL WHIP Whipped Topping, thawed

1 cup BAKER'S ANGEL FLAKE Coconut

▶ make it!

HEAT oven to 350°F.

1.  **PREPARE** cake batter in 2½-qt. ovenproof bowl as directed on package; scrape side of bowl. Beat cream cheese, egg and granulated sugar until well blended.

2.  **SPOON** into center of batter in bowl. Bake 1 hour 5 min. or until toothpick inserted in center comes out clean. Cool in bowl 10 min.

3.  **LOOSEN** cake from bowl with knife; invert onto wire rack. Remove bowl. Cool cake completely. Beat dry pudding mix, powdered sugar and milk in medium bowl with whisk 2 min.

4.  **STIR** in COOL WHIP. Refrigerate until ready to use. Place cake on plate; frost with pudding mixture. Cover with coconut. Keep refrigerated.

rugelach

PREP: 1 hr. | TOTAL: 25 hr. 25 min. (incl. refrigerating) | MAKES: about 5 doz. or 32 servings, 2 cookies each.

▶ what you need!

1 pkg. (8 oz.) PHILADELPHIA Cream Cheese, softened

1 cup (2 sticks) butter or margarine, softened

2¼ cups flour

1 cup finely chopped PLANTERS Walnuts

½ cup plus 2 Tbsp. sugar, divided

1 Tbsp. ground cinnamon, divided

¼ cup raspberry preserves

▶ make it!

1. **BEAT** cream cheese and butter in large bowl with mixer until well blended. Gradually add flour, mixing well after each addition. (Dough will be very soft and sticky.) Divide dough into 4 portions; place each on sheet of plastic wrap. Use floured hands to pat each portion into 1-inch-thick round. Wrap individually in plastic wrap. Refrigerate overnight.

2. **HEAT** oven to 325°F. Cover baking sheets with foil or parchment paper. Mix nuts, ½ cup sugar and 2 tsp. cinnamon. Roll each portion of dough to 11-inch circle on lightly floured surface; spread each with 1 Tbsp. preserves.

3. **SPRINKLE** nut mixture over preserves. Cut each circle into 16 wedges. Roll up each wedge, starting from wide side. Place, point-sides down, on prepared baking sheets; shape into crescents. Sprinkle with combined remaining sugar and cinnamon.

4. **BAKE** 25 min. or until lightly browned. Immediately remove from baking sheets to wire racks; cool completely.

wave-your-flag cheesecake

PREP: 20 min. plus refrigerating | MAKES: 20 servings.

▶ what you need!

4 cups strawberries, divided

1½ cups boiling water

2 pkg. (3 oz. each) JELL-O Brand Strawberry Flavor Gelatin

Ice cubes

1 cup cold water

1 pkg. (10.75 oz.) pound cake, cut into 10 slices

2 pkg. (8 oz. each) PHILADELPHIA Cream Cheese, softened

¼ cup sugar

1 tub (8 oz.) COOL WHIP Whipped Topping, thawed

1 cup blueberries

▶ make it!

1. **SLICE** 1 cup of the strawberries; set aside. Halve the remaining 3 cups strawberries; set aside. Stir boiling water into dry gelatin mixes in large bowl at least 2 min. until completely dissolved. Add enough ice to cold water to measure 2 cups. Add to gelatin; stir until ice is completely melted. Refrigerate 5 min. or until gelatin is slightly thickened (consistency of unbeaten egg whites).

2. **MEANWHILE,** line bottom of 13×9-inch dish with cake slices. Add sliced strawberries to thickened gelatin; stir gently. Spoon over cake slices. Refrigerate 4 hours or until set.

3. **BEAT** cream cheese and sugar in large bowl with wire whisk or electric mixer until well blended; gently stir in whipped topping. Spread over gelatin. Arrange strawberry halves on cream cheese mixture to resemble the stripes of a flag. Arrange blueberries on cream cheese mixture for the stars. Store any leftover dessert in refrigerator.

PHILADELPHIA 3-STEP mini cheesecake baskets

PREP: 10 min. | TOTAL: 2 hr. 30 min. | MAKES: 12 servings.

▶ what you need!

2 pkg. (8 oz. each) PHILADELPHIA Cream Cheese, softened

½ cup sugar

½ tsp. vanilla

2 eggs

12 NILLA Wafers

1½ cups BAKER'S ANGEL FLAKE Coconut, tinted green

36 small jelly beans

12 pieces shoestring licorice (4 inches each)

▶ make it!

HEAT oven to 350°F.

1. **BEAT** cream cheese, sugar and vanilla with electric mixer on medium speed until well blended. Add eggs; beat just until blended.

2. **PLACE** wafer on bottom of each of 12 paper-lined medium muffin cups. Spoon cream cheese mixture evenly over wafers.

3. **BAKE** 20 min. or until centers are almost set. Cool. Refrigerate at least 2 hours. Top evenly with coconut and jelly beans just before serving. Bend each licorice piece, then insert both ends into each cheesecake to resemble the handle of a basket. Store leftover cheesecakes in refrigerator.

HOW TO TINT COCONUT:
Place coconut and a few drops green food coloring in small resealable plastic bag. Seal bag. Shake bag gently until coconut is evenly tinted.

VARIATION:
Omit NILLA Wafers. Prepare as directed, pouring batter evenly into 12 ready-to-use single-serve graham cracker crumb crusts.

great pumpkin cake

PREP: 30 min. | TOTAL: 2 hr. 30 min. | MAKES: 24 servings.

▶ what you need!

1 pkg. (2-layer) cake mix, any flavor

1 pkg. (8 oz.) PHILADELPHIA Cream Cheese, softened

¼ cup (½ stick) butter, softened

4 cups powdered sugar

Few drops each: green, red and yellow food coloring

1 COMET Cup

▶ make it!

1. **PREPARE** cake batter and bake in 12-cup fluted tube pan as directed on package. Cool in pan 10 min. Invert cake onto wire rack; remove pan. Cool cake completely.

2. **MEANWHILE,** beat cream cheese and butter in medium bowl with electric mixer on medium speed until well blended. Gradually add sugar, beating until well blended after each addition. Remove ½ cup of the frosting; place in small bowl. Add green food coloring; stir until well blended. Spread half of the green frosting onto outside of ice cream cup; set aside. Cover and reserve remaining green frosting for later use.

3. **ADD** red and yellow food colorings to remaining white frosting to tint it orange. Spread onto cake to resemble pumpkin. Invert ice cream cup in hole in top of cake for the pumpkin's stem. Pipe the reserved green frosting in vertical lines down side of cake.

COOKING KNOW-HOW:
For a more rounded Great Pumpkin Cake, use a tall 12-cup fluted tube pan. As the cake bakes, it rises and forms a rounded top. When cake is unmolded (upside-down), the bottom of the cake will be rounded. If the cake is baked in a shorter 12-cup fluted tube pan, the resulting cake will be flatter.

FUN IDEA:
Place black gumdrops on sheet of waxed paper sprinkled with additional granulated sugar. Use a rolling pin to flatten each gumdrop, turning frequently to coat both sides with sugar. Cut into desired shapes with a sharp knife. Use to decorate frosted cake to resemble a jack-o'-lantern.

spider web pumpkin cheesecake

PREP: 15 min. | TOTAL: 4 hr. 10 min. (incl. refrigerating) | MAKES: 16 servings.

▶ what you need!

18 OREO Chocolate Sandwich Cookies, finely crushed (about 1½ cups)

2 Tbsp. butter or margarine, melted

3 pkg. (8 oz. each) PHILADELPHIA Cream Cheese, softened

¾ cup sugar

1 can (15 oz.) pumpkin

1 Tbsp. pumpkin pie spice

3 eggs

1 cup BREAKSTONE'S or KNUDSEN Sour Cream

1 square BAKER'S Semi-Sweet Chocolate

1 tsp. butter or margarine

▶ make it!

HEAT oven to 350°F.

1. **MIX** cookie crumbs and 2 Tbsp. butter; press onto bottom of 9-inch springform pan.

2. **BEAT** cream cheese and sugar in large bowl with electric mixer on medium speed until well blended. Add pumpkin and pumpkin pie spice; mix well. Add eggs, 1 at a time, mixing on low speed after each addition just until blended. Pour over crust.

3. **BAKE** 50 to 55 min. or until center is almost set; cool slightly. Carefully spread sour cream over top of cheesecake. Run knife or metal spatula around rim of pan to loosen cake; cool before removing rim of pan.

4. **PLACE** chocolate and 1 tsp. butter in small microwaveable bowl. Microwave on Medium (50%) 30 sec.; stir chocolate until completely melted; drizzle over cheesecake in spiral pattern. Starting at center of cheesecake, pull a toothpick through lines from center of cheesecake to outside edge to resemble a spider's web. Refrigerate 4 hours.

pumpkin spice frosted snack bars

PREP: 20 min. | TOTAL: 55 min. (incl. cooling) | MAKES: 24 servings.

▶ what you need!

1 pkg. (2-layer size) spice cake mix

1 can (15 oz.) pumpkin

1 cup MIRACLE WHIP Dressing

3 eggs

1 pkg. (8 oz.) PHILADELPHIA Cream Cheese, softened

¼ cup (½ stick) butter, softened

2 Tbsp. milk

1 tsp. vanilla

1 pkg. (16 oz.) powdered sugar (about 4 cups)

▶ make it!

HEAT oven to 350°F.

1. GREASE 13×9-inch baking pan; set aside. Beat cake mix, pumpkin, dressing and eggs in large bowl with electric mixer on medium speed until well blended. Pour into prepared pan.

2. BAKE 32 to 35 min. or until wooden toothpick inserted in center comes out clean. Cool completely in pan on wire rack.

3. BEAT cream cheese, butter, milk and vanilla in large bowl with electric mixer on medium speed until well blended. Gradually add sugar, beating after each addition until well blended. Spread over cooled cake. Cut into pieces to serve. Store any leftovers in refrigerator.

VARIATION:
Prepare as directed, using 15×10×1-inch baking pan and decreasing the baking time to 20 to 22 min. or until wooden toothpick inserted in center comes out clean.

chocolate cream ornament cake

PREP: 20 min. | TOTAL: 1 hr. 20 min. (incl. cooling) | MAKES: 16 servings, 1 slice each.

▶ what you need!

1 pkg. (2-layer size) chocolate cake mix

1 pkg. (3.9 oz.) JELL-O Chocolate Flavor Instant Pudding

1 pkg. (8 oz.) PHILADELPHIA Cream Cheese, softened

1 cup powdered sugar

1½ cups thawed COOL WHIP Whipped Topping

1 COMET Cup

1 piece red string licorice (2 inches)

Decorating gel

Colored sugar

▶ make it!

HEAT oven to 350°F.

1. **SPRAY** 2 (9-inch) round cake pans with cooking spray. Prepare cake batter as directed on package. Blend in dry pudding mix. Pour evenly into prepared pans.

2. **BAKE** as directed on package. Cool 10 min.; remove from pans to wire racks. Cool completely. Meanwhile, beat cream cheese and powdered sugar in small bowl with electric mixer on medium speed until well blended. Add whipped topping; stir until well blended.

3. **PLACE** 1 of the cake layers on serving plate; spread with one-third of the cream cheese mixture. Cover with remaining cake layer. Spread top and side of cake with remaining cream cheese mixture. Poke 2 small holes in bottom of ice cream cup; insert ends of licorice into holes leaving small loop at top. Place cup next to cake to resemble ornament hanger. Decorate top of cake with decorating gel and colored sugar as desired. Store in refrigerator.

EASY DECORATING IDEA:
For fun and easy patterns, place cookie cutters on top of cake and fill in shapes with colored sugar.

PHILADELPHIA
snowmen cookies

PREP: 20 min. | TOTAL: 41 min. | MAKES: about 3½ doz. or 44 servings, 2 cookies each.

▶ what you need!

1 pkg. (8 oz.) PHILADELPHIA Cream Cheese, softened

1 cup powdered sugar

¾ cup (1½ sticks) butter or margarine

½ tsp. vanilla

2 cups flour

½ tsp. baking soda

Suggested decorations: decorating gels, nonpareils, silver dragees

▶ make it!

HEAT oven to 325°F.

1. **BEAT** cream cheese, sugar, butter and vanilla with electric mixer on medium speed until well blended. Add flour and baking soda; mix well.

2. **SHAPE** dough into equal number of ½-inch and 1-inch diameter balls. (You should have about 44 of each size ball.) Using 1 small and 1 large ball for each snowman, place balls, slightly overlapping, on ungreased baking sheet. Flatten to ¼-inch thickness with bottom of glass dipped in additional flour. Repeat with remaining dough.

3. **BAKE** 19 to 21 minutes or until lightly browned. Cool on wire rack. Decorate as desired.

JAZZ IT UP:
Decorate with decorating gels, colored sprinkles and nonpareils to resemble snowmen. Cut peanut butter cups in half. Place 1 candy half on top of each snowman for hat.

HOW TO SOFTEN CREAM CHEESE:
Place completely unwrapped pkg. of cream cheese on microwaveable plate.
Microwave on HIGH 10 to 15 sec. or until slightly softened.

chocolate-raspberry thumbprints

PREP: 20 min. | TOTAL: 45 min. (incl. refrigerating) | MAKES: 4½ doz. or 27 servings, 2 cookies each.

▶ what you need!

2 cups flour

1 tsp. baking soda

¼ tsp. salt

4 squares BAKER'S Unsweetened Chocolate

½ cup (1 stick) butter

1 pkg. (8 oz.) PHILADELPHIA Cream Cheese, softened

1¼ cups sugar, divided

1 egg

1 tsp. vanilla

⅓ cup red raspberry jam

▶ make it!

HEAT oven to 375°F.

1. **MIX** flour, baking soda and salt; set aside. Microwave chocolate and butter in large microwaveable bowl on HIGH 2 min.; stir until chocolate is completely melted. Whisk in cream cheese. Add 1 cup sugar, egg and vanilla; mix well. Stir in flour mixture. Refrigerate 15 min.

2. **ROLL** dough into 1-inch balls; coat with remaining sugar. Place, 2 inches apart, on baking sheets. Press your thumb into center of each ball; fill each indentation with about ¼ tsp. jam.

3. **BAKE** 8 to 10 min. or until lightly browned. Cool 1 min. on baking sheet; transfer to wire racks. Cool completely.

key lime cheesecake pie

PREP: 25 min. | TOTAL: 8 hr. 25 min. (incl. refrigerating) | MAKES: 10 servings.

▶ what you need!

1¼ cups finely crushed coconut bar cookies

¼ cup (½ stick) butter or margarine, melted

3 Tbsp. sugar

2 pkg. (8 oz. each) PHILADELPHIA Cream Cheese, softened

1 can (14 oz.) sweetened condensed milk

½ tsp. grated lime peel

⅓ cup lime juice

Few drops green food coloring (optional)

▶ make it!

HEAT oven to 350°F.

1. **MIX** crumbs, butter and sugar; press firmly onto bottom and up side of 9-inch pie plate. Bake 10 min. Cool.

2. **BEAT** cream cheese and sweetened condensed milk in large bowl with electric mixer on medium speed until well blended. Add peel, juice and food coloring, if desired; mix well. Pour into crust.

3. **REFRIGERATE** at least 8 hours or overnight. Store leftover pie in refrigerator.

SPECIAL EXTRA:
Garnish with lime slices and fresh mint just before serving.

summer berry trifle

PREP: 40 min. plus refrigerating | MAKES: 18 servings.

▶ what you need!

1 cup boiling water

1 pkg. (6 oz.) JELL-O Strawberry Flavor Gelatin

Ice cubes

½ cup cold water

2 cups mixed fresh berries (raspberries, blueberries, halved strawberries)

1 pkg. (8 oz.) PHILADELPHIA Cream Cheese, softened

1¼ cups cold milk, divided

1 pkg. (3.4 oz.) JELL-O Cheesecake or Vanilla Flavor Instant Pudding

1 tub (8 oz.) COOL WHIP Strawberry Whipped Topping, thawed

1 pkg. (12 oz.) pound cake, cubed

▶ make it!

1. **STIR** boiling water into dry gelatin in large bowl at least 2 min. until completely dissolved. Add enough ice to cold water to measure 1 cup. Add to gelatin; stir until ice is completely melted. Let stand about 15 min. or until thickened. (Spoon drawn through gelatin leaves definite impression.) Stir in berries.

2. **PLACE** cream cheese in large bowl; beat with wire whisk until creamy. Gradually add ¼ cup of the milk, beating until well blended. Add remaining 1 cup milk and dry pudding mix; beat 2 min. or until well blended. Gently stir in whipped topping. Set aside.

3. **PLACE** about half of the cake cubes in bottom of large serving bowl; cover with half of the pudding mixture. Top with layers of the gelatin mixture, remaining cake cubes and remaining pudding mixture. Refrigerate at least 1 hour. Garnish as desired. Store leftover dessert in refrigerator.

striped delight

PREP: 20 min. | TOTAL: 4 hr. 40 min. (incl. refrigerating) | MAKES: 24 servings.

▶ what you need!

35 OREO Cookies

6 Tbsp. butter, melted

1 pkg. (8 oz.) PHILADELPHIA Cream Cheese, softened

¼ cup sugar

2 Tbsp. cold milk

1 tub (12 oz.) COOL WHIP Whipped Topping, thawed, divided

2 pkg. (3.9 oz. each) JELL-O Chocolate Instant Pudding

3¼ cups cold milk

▶ make it!

1. **PROCESS** cookies in food processor until fine crumbs form. Transfer to medium bowl; mix in butter. Press onto bottom of 13×9-inch dish. Refrigerate until ready to use.

2. **WHISK** cream cheese, sugar and 2 Tbsp. milk in medium bowl until blended. Stir in 1¼ cups COOL WHIP; spread over crust.

3. **BEAT** pudding mixes and 3¼ cups milk with whisk 2 min.; pour over cream cheese layer. Let stand 5 min. or until thickened; cover with remaining COOL WHIP. Refrigerate 4 hours.

HOW TO EASILY CUT DESSERT INTO SQUARES:
Place dessert in freezer about 1 hour before cutting into squares to serve.

SPECIAL EXTRA:
Drizzle each plate with melted BAKER'S Semi-Sweet Chocolate before topping with dessert square. Sprinkle with crushed candy canes or additional crushed OREO Cookies.

rustic fall fruit tart

PREP: 15 min. | TOTAL: 1 hr. 45 min. (incl. refrigerating) | MAKES: 8 servings.

▸ what you need!

1½ cups flour

½ cup (1 stick) butter, softened

½ cup (½ of 8-oz. container) PHILADELPHIA Cream Cheese Spread

4 medium plums, thinly sliced

2 medium nectarines, thinly sliced

⅓ cup sugar

1 tsp. ground ginger

1 Tbsp. cornstarch

⅓ cup apricot jam

▸ make it!

1. **PLACE** flour, butter and cream cheese in food processor container; cover. Process, using pulsing action, until mixture is well blended and almost forms a ball. Shape dough into ball; wrap tightly with plastic wrap. Refrigerate 1 hour or until chilled.

2. **HEAT** oven to 400°F. Place pastry on lightly floured surface; roll out to 12-inch circle. Place on lightly greased baking sheet; set aside. Toss fruit with sugar, ginger and cornstarch. Arrange decoratively over crust to within 2 inches of edge of crust. Fold edge of crust over fruit.

3. **BAKE** 30 min. Remove from oven; spread fruit with jam. Serve warm or at room temperature.

Showstopping
Desserts

DESSERTS TO IMPRESS YOUR GUESTS

strawberry freeze

PREP: 15 min. plus freezing | MAKES: 16 servings.

▶ what you need!

12 CHIPS AHOY! Cookies

1 pkg. (8 oz.) PHILADELPHIA Cream Cheese, softened

½ cup sugar

1 can (12 oz.) frozen berry juice concentrate, thawed

1 cup crushed strawberries

1 tub (8 oz.) COOL WHIP Whipped Topping, thawed

2 cups whole strawberries, cut in half

▶ make it!

1. **ARRANGE** cookies in single layer on bottom of 9-inch springform pan.

2. **BEAT** cream cheese and sugar with mixer until well blended. Gradually beat in juice concentrate. Stir in crushed strawberries. Whisk in COOL WHIP until well blended. Pour over cookies in pan.

3. **FREEZE** 6 hours or until firm. Remove from freezer 15 min. before serving; let stand at room temperature to soften slightly. Top with berry halves just before serving.

SUBSTITUTE:
Prepare using COOL WHIP DIPS Strawberry Créme.

layered strawberry cheesecake bowl

PREP: 20 min. plus refrigerating | MAKES: 14 servings, ⅔ cup each.

▶ what you need!

3 cups sliced fresh strawberries

3 Tbsp. sugar

2 pkg. (8 oz. each) PHILADELPHIA Neufchâtel Cheese, softened

1½ cups cold milk

1 pkg. (3.4 oz.) JELL-O Vanilla Flavor Instant Pudding

2 cups thawed COOL WHIP LITE Whipped Topping, divided

2 cups frozen pound cake cubes (1 inch)

1 square BAKER'S Semi-Sweet Chocolate

▶ make it!

1. **COMBINE** berries and sugar; refrigerate until ready to use. Beat Neufchâtel with mixer until creamy. Gradually beat in milk. Add dry pudding mix; mix well.

2. **BLEND** in 1½ cups COOL WHIP. Spoon half into 2½-qt. bowl.

3. **TOP** with layers of cake, berries and remaining Neufchâtel mixture. Refrigerate 4 hours.

4. **MELT** chocolate; drizzle over trifle. Top with remaining COOL WHIP.

SPECIAL EXTRA:
Garnish with chocolate-covered strawberries just before serving.

NOTE:
You will need about half of a 10.75-oz. pkg. pound cake to get the 4 cups cake cubes needed to prepare this recipe.

banana-sour cream cake

PREP: 15 min. | TOTAL: 1 hr. 50 min. (incl. cooling) | MAKES: 16 servings.

▶ what you need!

1 pkg. (2-layer size) yellow cake mix

3 eggs

1 cup mashed ripe bananas (about 3)

1 cup BREAKSTONE'S or KNUDSEN Sour Cream

¼ cup oil

1 pkg. (8 oz.) PHILADELPHIA Cream Cheese, softened

½ cup (1 stick) butter, softened

1 pkg. (16 oz.) powdered sugar

1 cup finely chopped PLANTERS Walnuts

▶ make it!

HEAT oven to 350°F.

1. **BEAT** first 5 ingredients with mixer on low speed just until moistened, stopping frequently to scrape bottom and side of bowl. Beat on medium speed 2 min. Pour into greased and floured 13×9-inch pan.

2. **BAKE** 35 min. or until toothpick inserted in center comes out clean. Cool completely.

3. **BEAT** cream cheese and butter with mixer until well blended. Gradually add sugar, beating well after each addition.

4. **REMOVE** cake from pan. Carefully cut cake crosswise in half using serrated knife. Place 1 cake half, top-side down, on plate; spread with some of the cream cheese frosting. Top with remaining cake half, top-side up. Spread top and sides with remaining frosting. Press nuts into sides. Keep refrigerated.

SUBSTITUTE:
Prepare using BREAKSTONE'S Reduced Fat or KNUDSEN Light Sour Cream.

cookies & cream freeze

PREP: 30 min. plus freezing | MAKES: 12 servings.

▶ what you need!

4 squares BAKER'S Semi-Sweet Chocolate

14 OREO Chocolate Sandwich Cookies, divided

1 pkg. (8 oz.) PHILADELPHIA Cream Cheese, softened

¼ cup sugar

½ tsp. vanilla

1 tub (8 oz.) COOL WHIP Whipped Topping, thawed

▶ make it!

1. **MELT** chocolate as directed on package; set aside until ready to use. Line 8½×4½-inch loaf pan with foil, with ends of foil extending over sides of pan. Arrange 8 of the cookies evenly on bottom of pan. Crumble remaining 6 cookies; set aside.

2. **BEAT** cream cheese, sugar and vanilla in medium bowl with electric mixer until well blended. Stir in whipped topping. Remove about 1½ cups of the cream cheese mixture; place in medium bowl. Stir in melted chocolate.

3. **SPREAD** remaining cream cheese mixture over cookies in pan; sprinkle with crumbled cookies. Gently press cookies into cream cheese mixture with back of spoon; top with chocolate mixture. Cover. Freeze 3 hours or until firm. Remove from freezer about 15 min. before serving; invert onto serving plate. Peel off foil; let stand at room temperature to soften slightly before cutting to serve.

JAZZ IT UP:
Drizzle serving plates with additional melted BAKER'S Semi-Sweet Chocolate for a spectacular, yet simple, dessert presentation.

cafe ladyfinger dessert

PREP: 20 min. plus refrigerating | MAKES: 12 servings.

▶ what you need!

2 pkg. (3 oz. each) ladyfingers, split, separated

1 cup freshly brewed strong MAXWELL HOUSE Coffee or YUBAN
    Coffee, any variety, at room temperature, divided

1 pkg. (8 oz.) PHILADELPHIA Fat Free Cream Cheese

2 cups cold fat-free milk

2 pkg. (1.5 oz. each) JELL-O Vanilla Flavor Fat Free Sugar Free Instant
    Reduced Calorie Pudding

1 tub (8 oz.) COOL WHIP FREE Whipped Topping, thawed, divided

▶ make it!

1. **BRUSH** cut side of ladyfingers with about ¼ cup of the coffee. Place ladyfingers on bottom and up side of 2-quart serving bowl.

2. **BEAT** cream cheese and remaining ¾ cup coffee in large bowl with wire whisk until smooth. Gradually beat in milk until smooth. Add pudding mixes. Beat with wire whisk until blended. Gently stir in half of the whipped topping. Spoon into prepared bowl; cover.

3. **REFRIGERATE** 1 hour or until ready to serve. Top with remaining whipped topping.

SHORTCUT:
Substitute 2 tsp. MAXWELL HOUSE Instant Coffee, dissolved in 1 cup hot water, for freshly brewed coffee.

PHILADELPHIA
cherry danish dessert

PREP: 15 min. | TOTAL: 1 hr. (incl. cooling) | MAKES: 24 servings, 1 rectangle each.

▶ what you need!

2 cans (8 oz. each) refrigerated crescent dinner rolls, divided

2 pkg. (8 oz. each) PHILADELPHIA Cream Cheese, softened

1½ cups powdered sugar, divided

1 egg white

1 tsp. vanilla

1 can (21 oz.) cherry pie filling

3 Tbsp. milk

▶ make it!

HEAT oven to 350°F.

1. **UNROLL** 1 of the cans of crescent dough into 2 long rectangles. Place in greased 13×9-inch baking pan; press onto bottom of pan to form crust, firmly pressing seams together to seal.

2. **BEAT** cream cheese, ¾ cup of the sugar, the egg white and vanilla with electric mixer on medium speed until well blended. Spread onto crust; cover with pie filling. Unroll remaining can of crescent dough; separate into 2 long rectangles. Pat out to form 13×9-inch rectangle, pressing seams together to seal. Place over pie filling to form top crust.

3. **BAKE** 25 to 30 min. or until golden brown; cool slightly. Gradually add milk to remaining ¾ cup sugar, beating with wire whisk until well blended. Drizzle over warm dessert. Cut into 24 rectangles to serve. Store leftover dessert in refrigerator.

VARIATION:
Prepare as directed, using apricot or raspberry pie filling. Or, substitute 2 cups chocolate chips or your favorite chopped PLANTERS Nuts for the pie filling.

SUBSTITUTE:
Prepare as directed, using 2 tubs (8 oz. each) PHILADELPHIA Cream Cheese Spread and fat-free milk.

chocolate mousse torte

PREP: 20 min. plus refrigerating | MAKES: 16 servings.

▶ what you need!

37 NILLA Wafers, divided

4 squares BAKER'S Semi-Sweet Chocolate, divided

2 pkg. (3.9 oz. each) JELL-O Chocolate Instant Pudding

2 cups plus 2 Tbsp. cold milk, divided

1 tub (8 oz.) COOL WHIP Whipped Topping, thawed, divided

1 pkg. (8 oz.) PHILADELPHIA Cream Cheese, softened

¼ cup sugar

¾ cup fresh raspberries

▶ make it!

1.  STAND 16 wafers around inside edge of 9-inch round pan lined with plastic wrap. Melt 3 chocolate squares as directed on package.

2.  BEAT pudding mixes and 2 cups milk with whisk 2 min. Add melted chocolate; mix well. Stir in 1 cup COOL WHIP; pour into prepared pan. Beat cream cheese, sugar and remaining milk with mixer until well blended.

3.  STIR in 1 cup of the remaining COOL WHIP; spread over pudding. Top with remaining wafers. Refrigerate 3 hours.

4.  MEANWHILE, shave remaining chocolate square into curls. Invert torte onto plate. Remove pan and plastic wrap. Top torte with remaining COOL WHIP, berries and chocolate curls.

red velvet cake

PREP: 10 min. | TOTAL: 2 hr. 45 min. (incl. cooling) | MAKES: 16 servings.

▶ what you need!

1 pkg. (2-layer size) white cake mix

2 squares BAKER'S Unsweetened Chocolate, melted

1 Tbsp. red food coloring

1 pkg. (8 oz.) PHILADELPHIA Cream Cheese, softened

½ cup (1 stick) butter or margarine, melted

1 pkg. (16 oz.) powdered sugar (about 4 cups)

½ cup chopped PLANTERS Pecans

▶ make it!

1. **PREPARE** and bake cake mix as directed on package for 2 (9-inch) round cake layers, adding chocolate and food coloring with water, eggs and oil; cool completely.

2. **BEAT** cream cheese and butter with electric mixer on medium speed until well blended. Gradually add sugar, beating well after each addition. Stir in pecans.

3. **FILL** and frost cake layers with cream cheese frosting.

Chinese Noo

caramel-pecan cheesecake bars

PREP: 15 min. plus refrigerating | TOTAL: 5 hr. 5 min. (incl. refrigerating) | MAKES: 32 servings.

▸ what you need!

½ cup NABISCO Graham Cracker Crumbs

1 cup coarsely chopped PLANTERS Pecans, divided

2 Tbsp. granulated sugar

¼ cup (½ stick) butter, melted

4 pkg. (8 oz. each) PHILADELPHIA Cream Cheese, softened

1 cup firmly packed brown sugar

2 Tbsp. flour

½ cup BREAKSTONE'S or KNUDSEN Sour Cream

1 Tbsp. vanilla

3 eggs

1 bag (14 oz.) KRAFT Caramels, divided

▸ make it!

HEAT oven to 350°F.

1. **LINE** 13×9-inch baking pan with foil, with ends of foil extending over sides of pan. Mix graham crumbs, ½ cup pecans, granulated sugar and butter; press firmly onto bottom of prepared pan. Bake 10 min.

2. **BEAT** cream cheese, brown sugar and flour in large bowl with electric mixer on medium speed until well blended. Add sour cream and vanilla; mix well. Add eggs, 1 at a time, mixing on low speed after each addition just until blended. Place 36 of the caramels and 1 Tbsp. water in microwaveable bowl. Microwave on HIGH 1 min. or until caramels are completely melted when stirred. Add to cream cheese batter; stir until well blended. Pour over crust.

3. **BAKE** 40 min. or until center is almost set. Sprinkle cheesecake with remaining ½ cup pecans. Refrigerate at least 4 hours or overnight.

4. **PLACE** remaining caramels and additional 1 Tbsp. water in microwaveable bowl. Microwave on HIGH 1 min. or until caramels are completely melted when stirred. Drizzle over cheesecake; let stand until set. Remove dessert from pan using foil handles; cut into 32 bars to serve. Store leftover bars in refrigerator.

chocolate ribbon pie

PREP: 15 min. plus refrigerating | MAKES: 8 servings.

▸ what you need!

4 oz. (½ of 8-oz. pkg.) PHILADELPHIA Cream Cheese, softened

2 Tbsp. sugar

2 cups plus 1 Tbsp. milk, divided

1 tub (8 oz.) COOL WHIP Whipped Topping, thawed, divided

1 OREO Pie Crust (6 oz.)

2 pkg. (3.9 oz. each) JELL-O Chocolate Instant Pudding

▸ make it!

1. **BEAT** cream cheese, sugar and 1 Tbsp. milk in medium bowl with whisk until well blended. Stir in half the COOL WHIP; spread onto bottom of crust.

2. **BEAT** pudding mixes and remaining milk with whisk 2 min. (Mixture will be thick.) Pour over layer in crust.

3. **REFRIGERATE** 4 hours or until firm. Top with remaining COOL WHIP just before serving.

chocolate & peanut butter ribbon dessert

PREP: 15 min. plus freezing | MAKES: 12 servings.

▶ what you need!

12 NUTTER BUTTER Peanut Butter Sandwich Cookies, divided

2 Tbsp. butter, melted

1 pkg. (8 oz.) PHILADELPHIA Cream Cheese, softened

½ cup creamy peanut butter

½ cup sugar

2 tsp. vanilla

1 tub (12 oz.) COOL WHIP Whipped Topping, thawed, divided

2 squares BAKER'S Semi-Sweet Chocolate, melted

▶ make it!

1. **CRUSH** 8 cookies; mix with butter. Press onto bottom of foil-lined 9×5-inch loaf pan.

2. **MIX** next 4 ingredients with mixer until well blended. Whisk in 3 cups COOL WHIP; spoon ½ cup into small bowl. Blend in melted chocolate. Spoon half the remaining cream cheese mixture over crust; top with layers of chocolate mixture and remaining cream cheese mixture.

3. **FREEZE** 4 hours or until firm. Invert onto plate. Remove foil, then re-invert dessert onto serving platter so crumb layer is on bottom. Coarsely break remaining cookies. Top dessert with remaining COOL WHIP and cookies.

MAKE AHEAD:
Dessert can be frozen overnight before unmolding and serving as directed.

fast & easy tiramisu

PREP: 15 min. plus refrigerating | MAKES: 12 servings.

▶ what you need!

2 pkg. (3 oz. each) ladyfingers, split, divided

2 Tbsp. MAXWELL HOUSE Instant Coffee

1 Tbsp. sugar

1 cup boiling water

2 pkg. (8 oz. each) PHILADELPHIA Fat Free Cream Cheese, softened

½ cup sugar

2 cups thawed COOL WHIP LITE Whipped Topping

1 tsp. unsweetened cocoa powder

▶ make it!

1. **ARRANGE** 1 pkg. of ladyfingers on bottom of 13×9-inch baking dish. Dissolve combined coffee granules and 1 Tbsp. sugar in boiling water; brush ½ cup onto ladyfingers in dish.

2. **BEAT** cream cheese in large bowl with mixer until creamy. Add ½ cup sugar; mix well. Whisk in COOL WHIP.

3. **SPREAD** half the cream cheese mixture over ladyfingers in dish; top with remaining ladyfingers. Brush with remaining coffee mixture; cover with remaining cream cheese mixture. Sprinkle with cocoa powder. Refrigerate 4 hours.

SPECIAL EXTRA:
Add 2 Tbsp. almond-flavored liqueur or brandy to cream cheese along with the ½ cup sugar.

shortcut carrot cake

PREP: 30 min. | TOTAL: 1 hr. 30 min. (incl. cooling) | MAKES: 18 servings.

▶ what you need!

1 pkg. (2-layer size) spice cake mix

2 cups shredded carrots (about 3 large)

1 can (8 oz.) crushed pineapple, drained

1 cup chopped PLANTERS Pecans, divided

2 pkg. (8 oz. each) PHILADELPHIA Cream Cheese, softened

2 cups powdered sugar

1 tub (8 oz.) COOL WHIP Whipped Topping, thawed

▶ make it!

HEAT oven to 350°F.

1. **PREPARE** cake batter as directed on package; stir in carrots, pineapple and ¾ cup nuts. Pour into 2 (9-inch) square pans. Bake 25 to 30 min. or until toothpick inserted in centers comes out clean. Cool in pans 10 min.; invert onto wire racks. Remove pans. Turn cakes over; cool completely.

2. **MEANWHILE,** beat cream cheese and sugar until well blended. Whisk in COOL WHIP.

3. **STACK** cake layers on plate, spreading frosting between layers and on top and sides of cake. Top with remaining nuts. Keep refrigerated.

FOR A DECORATIVE DESIGN:
Use a toothpick to draw 4 diagonal lines across top of cake; sprinkle remaining ¼ cup nuts over lines.

SUBSTITUTE:
Substitute a yellow cake mix plus 2 tsp. ground cinnamon for the spice cake mix.

PHILADELPHIA 3-STEP double-chocolate layer cheesecake

PREP: 10 min. plus refrigerating | TOTAL: 4 hr. 50 min. (inc;. refrigerating) | MAKES: 8 servings.

▶ what you need!

2 pkg. (8 oz. each) PHILADELPHIA Cream Cheese, softened

½ cup sugar

½ tsp. vanilla

2 eggs

3 squares BAKER'S Semi-Sweet Chocolate, melted, cooled slightly

1 OREO Pie Crust (6 oz.)

½ cup thawed COOL WHIP Whipped Topping

4 fresh strawberries, halved

▶ make it!

HEAT oven to 350°F.

1. **BEAT** cream cheese, sugar and vanilla in large bowl with electric mixer on medium speed until well blended. Add eggs, 1 at a time, beating on low speed after each addition just until blended.

2. **REMOVE** 1 cup of the batter to small bowl; stir in melted chocolate. Pour into crust; top with remaining plain batter.

3. **BAKE** 40 min. or until center is almost set. Cool. Refrigerate 3 hours or overnight. Top with whipped topping and strawberries just before serving. Store leftover cheesecake in refrigerator.

PHILADELPHIA 3-STEP
crème de menthe cheesecake

PREP: 10 min. | TOTAL: 4 hr. 50 min. (incl. refrigerating) | MAKES: 8 servings.

▶ what you need!

2 pkg. (8 oz. each) PHILADELPHIA Cream Cheese, softened

½ cup granulated sugar

½ tsp. vanilla

2 eggs

4 tsp. green crème de menthe

1 OREO Pie Crust (6 oz.)

2 tsp. green cake decorating crystals or colored sugar

▶ make it!

HEAT oven to 350°F.

1. **BEAT** cream cheese, granulated sugar and vanilla with electric mixer on medium speed until well blended. Add eggs; mix well. Stir in crème de menthe.

2. **POUR** into crust.

3. **BAKE** 40 min. or until center is almost set. Cool. Refrigerate 3 hours or overnight. Sprinkle with decorating crystals just before serving. Store leftover cheesecake in refrigerator.

ALMOND-CHERRY CHEESECAKE:
Prepare as directed, substituting 2 Tbsp. almond-flavored liqueur for the crème de menthe and using a HONEY MAID Graham Pie Crust. Top with 1 can (21 oz.) cherry pie filling just before serving.

tiramisu bowl

PREP: 20 min. plus refrigerating | MAKES: 16 servings, about ⅔ cup each.

▶ what you need!

1 pkg. (8 oz.) PHILADELPHIA Cream Cheese, softened

3 cups cold milk

2 pkg. (3.4 oz. each) JELL-O Vanilla Flavor Instant Pudding

1 tub (8 oz.) COOL WHIP Whipped Topping, thawed, divided

48 NILLA Wafers

½ cup brewed strong MAXWELL HOUSE Coffee, cooled

2 squares BAKER'S Semi-Sweet Chocolate, coarsely grated

1 cup fresh raspberries

▶ make it!

1. **BEAT** cream cheese in large bowl with electric mixer until creamy. Gradually beat in milk. Add dry pudding mixes; mix well. Stir in 2 cups of the whipped topping.

2. **LINE** bottom and side of a 2½-qt. bowl with half of the wafers; drizzle with half of the coffee. Layer half of the pudding mixture over wafers, and then top with half of the grated chocolate. Repeat all layers starting with the wafers and coffee. Top with remaining whipped topping and raspberries.

3. **REFRIGERATE** at least 2 hours. Store leftovers in refrigerator.

cream cheese flan

PREP: 20 min. | TOTAL: 4 hr. 50 min. (incl. refrigerating) | MAKES: 8 servings.

▶ what you need!

2 cups sugar, divided

1 can (12 oz.) evaporated milk

1 pkg. (8 oz.) PHILADELPHIA Cream Cheese, cubed, softened

5 eggs

1 tsp. vanilla

Dash salt

▶ make it!

HEAT oven to 350°F.

1. **COOK** 1 cup sugar in small saucepan on medium heat until sugar is melted and deep golden brown, stirring constantly. Pour into 9-inch round pan; tilt pan to cover bottom with syrup.

2. **BLEND** milk and cream cheese in blender until smooth. Add remaining sugar, eggs, vanilla and salt; blend just until smooth. Pour over syrup in pan. Place filled pan in larger pan; add enough hot water to larger pan to come halfway up side of smaller pan.

3. **BAKE** 50 min. to 1 hour or until knife inserted near center comes out clean. Cool slightly. Carefully remove flan from water. Cool completely on wire rack. Refrigerate several hours or until chilled. Unmold onto plate just before serving.

FLAVOR VARIATIONS:
Prepare as directed. Choose one of the following options:
Guava: Add ½ cup guava paste, cut into pieces, or ½ cup canned guava shells in heavy syrup to cream cheese batter before pouring into prepared pan.
Lime: Add zest from 1 lime to boiling sugar mixture; remove from syrup before sugar caramelizes. Pour into prepared pan as directed.
Cajeta: Add ¼ cup cajeta (Mexican goat milk caramel) to cream cheese batter before pouring into prepared pan.
Chocolate-Orange: Add 2 squares BAKER'S Semi-Sweet Chocolate, melted and cooled, and 1 Tbsp. orange zest to cream cheese batter before pouring into prepared pan.
Coconut: Omit vanilla and add ¼ cup BAKER'S ANGEL FLAKE Coconut or ½ cup coconut milk and 1 Tbsp. rum to cream cheese batter before pouring into prepared pan.

SPECIAL EXTRA:
Garnish with fresh berries just before serving.

triple-berry cheesecake tart

PREP: 15 min. plus refrigerating | MAKES: 10 servings.

▶ what you need!

45 NILLA Wafers, finely crushed (about 1¼ cups)

¼ cup (½ stick) butter, melted

1 pkg. (8 oz.) PHILADELPHIA Cream Cheese, softened

¼ cup sugar

1 cup thawed COOL WHIP Whipped Topping

2 cups mixed berries (raspberries, sliced strawberries and blueberries)

¾ cup boiling water

1 pkg. (3 oz.) JELL-O Brand Lemon Flavor Gelatin

1 cup ice cubes

▶ make it!

1. **MIX** wafer crumbs and butter in small bowl until well blended. Press onto bottom and up side of 9-inch tart pan. Place in freezer while preparing filling.

2. **BEAT** cream cheese and sugar in large bowl with electric mixer on medium speed until well blended. Gently stir in whipped topping. Spoon into crust; top with berries. Cover and refrigerate.

3. **STIR** boiling water into dry gelatin mix in medium bowl 2 min. until completely dissolved. Add ice cubes; stir until ice is completely melted. Refrigerate about 15 min. or until slightly thickened (consistency of unbeaten egg whites). Spoon gelatin over fruit in pan. Refrigerate 3 hours.

Kids' Favorites

TREATS KIDS LOVE TO MAKE AND EAT

mini OREO
surprise cupcakes

PREP: 10 min. | TOTAL: 52 min. (incl. cooling) | MAKES: 24 servings.

▶ what you need!

1 pkg. (2-layer size) chocolate cake mix

1 pkg. (8 oz.) PHILADELPHIA Cream Cheese, softened

1 egg

2 Tbsp. sugar

48 Mini OREO Bite Size Chocolate Sandwich Cookies

1½ cups thawed COOL WHIP Whipped Topping

▶ make it!

HEAT oven to 350°F.

1. **PREPARE** cake batter as directed on package; set aside. Beat cream cheese, egg and sugar until well blended.

2. **SPOON** cake batter into 24 paper- or foil-lined 2½-inch muffin cups, filling each cup about half full. Top each with about 1½ tsp. of the cream cheese mixture and 1 cookie. Cover evenly with remaining cake batter.

3. **BAKE** 19 to 22 min. or until wooden toothpick inserted in centers comes out clean. Cool 5 min.; remove from pans to wire racks. Cool completely. (There may be an indentation in top of each cupcake after baking.) Top cupcakes with whipped topping and remaining cookies just before serving. Store in tightly covered container in refrigerator up to 3 days.

MAKE IT EASY:
For easy portioning of cream cheese mixture into cake batter, spoon cream cheese mixture into large resealable plastic bag. Seal bag securely. Snip small corner of bag with scissors. Squeeze about 1½ tsp. of the cream cheese mixture over batter in each muffin cup.

cherries in the snow

PREP: 10 min. I MAKES: 8 servings.

▶ what you need!

1 pkg. (8 oz.) PHILADELPHIA Cream Cheese, softened

½ cup sugar

2 cups thawed COOL WHIP Whipped Topping

1 can (21 oz.) cherry pie filling, divided

▶ make it!

1. **MIX** cream cheese and sugar until well blended. Stir in whipped topping.

2. **LAYER** heaping 2 Tbsp. cream cheese mixture and 2 Tbsp. pie filling in each of 8 stemmed glasses or dessert dishes. Repeat layers.

3. **STORE** leftovers in refrigerator.

VARIATION:
Prepare as directed, using PHILADELPHIA Neufchâtel Cheese and COOL WHIP LITE Whipped Topping.

STORAGE KNOW-HOW:
Once thawed, refrigerate COOL WHIP Whipped Topping for up to 2 weeks or re-freeze.

cinnamon toast "blinis"

PREP: 20 min. | TOTAL: 35 min. | MAKES: 18 servings.

▶ what you need!

1 pkg. (8 oz.) PHILADELPHIA Cream Cheese, softened

½ cup sugar, divided

¼ tsp. vanilla

1 egg yolk

1 tsp. ground cinnamon

12 slices white bread, crusts removed

3 Tbsp. butter or margarine, melted

▶ make it!

HEAT oven to 400°F.

1. **BEAT** cream cheese, ¼ cup sugar, vanilla and egg yolk with whisk until well blended. In separate bowl, mix remaining sugar and cinnamon.

2. **FLATTEN** bread slices with rolling pin. Spread each with 1 rounded Tbsp. cream cheese mixture; roll up tightly, starting at 1 short end. Brush with butter; roll in reserved cinnamon-sugar. Cut each roll into 3 pieces; place, seam-sides down, on baking sheet.

3. **BAKE** 12 to 15 min. or until edges are lightly browned. Serve warm.

Rolls can
be prepared
ahead of time and
kept frozen until
ready to slice
and bake.

peanut butter cup pie

PREP: 15 min. plus refrigerating | MAKES: 10 servings.

▶ what you need!

1 pkg. (8 oz.) PHILADELPHIA Cream Cheese, softened

½ cup plus 1 Tbsp. creamy peanut butter, divided

1 cup cold milk

1 pkg. (3.9 oz.) JELL-O Vanilla Flavor Instant Pudding

2½ cups thawed COOL WHIP Whipped Topping, divided

1 OREO Pie Crust (6 oz.)

3 squares BAKER'S Semi-Sweet Chocolate

▶ make it!

1. **BEAT** cream cheese and ½ cup peanut butter until well blended. Add milk and dry pudding mix; beat 2 min. Whisk in 1 cup COOL WHIP; spoon into crust. Refrigerate until ready to use.

2. **MEANWHILE,** microwave remaining COOL WHIP and chocolate in microwaveable bowl on HIGH 1½ to 2 min. or until chocolate is completely melted and mixture is well blended, stirring after each minute. Cool completely.

3. **SPREAD** chocolate mixture over pudding layer in crust. Microwave remaining peanut butter in small microwaveable bowl 30 sec.; stir. Drizzle over pie. Refrigerate 4 hours or until firm.

SUBSTITUTE:
Prepare using 1 pkg. (3.9 oz.) JELL-O Chocolate Instant Pudding.

red velvet cupcakes

PREP: 15 min. | TOTAL: 1 hr. 10 min. (incl. cooling) | MAKES: 24 servings.

▶ what you need!

1 pkg. (2-layer size) red velvet cake mix

1 pkg. (3.9 oz.) JELL-O Chocolate Instant Pudding

1 pkg. (8 oz.) PHILADELPHIA Cream Cheese, softened

½ cup (1 stick) butter or margarine, softened

1 pkg. (16 oz.) powdered sugar (about 4 cups)

1 cup thawed COOL WHIP Whipped Topping

1 square BAKER'S White Chocolate, shaved into curls

▶ make it!

HEAT oven to 325°F.

1.

2.

3.

PREPARE cake batter and bake as directed on package for 24 cupcakes, blending dry pudding mix into batter before spooning into prepared muffin cups. Cool.

MEANWHILE, beat cream cheese and butter in large bowl with mixer until well blended. Gradually beat in sugar. Whisk in COOL WHIP; spoon 1½ cups into resealable plastic bag. Seal bag; cut 1 small corner off bottom of bag. Use to squeeze 1 Tbsp. cream cheese frosting into center of each cupcake.

FROST cupcakes with remaining frosting. Top with chocolate curls. Keep refrigerated.

CHIPS AHOY!
cheesecake sandwiches

PREP: 10 min. plus freezing | MAKES: 10 servings.

▶ what you need!

4 oz. (½ of 8-oz. pkg.) PHILADELPHIA Cream Cheese, softened

2 Tbsp. sugar

1 cup thawed COOL WHIP Whipped Topping

20 CHIPS AHOY! Real Chocolate Chip Cookies

1 tub (7 oz.) BAKER'S Milk Chocolate Dipping Chocolate, melted

▶ make it!

1. **BEAT** cream cheese and sugar in large bowl with electric mixer on medium speed until well blended. Stir in whipped topping.

2. **COVER** bottom (flat) side of each of 10 of the cookies with about 2 Tbsp. of the cream cheese mixture; top each with second cookie, bottom-side down, to form sandwich. Dip half of each sandwich in chocolate; gently shake off excess chocolate. Place in single layer in airtight container.

3. **FREEZE** 3 hours or until firm. Store leftover sandwiches in freezer.

PHILADELPHIA 3-STEP
cheesecake bars

PREP: 10 min.| TOTAL: 4 hr. 50 min. (incl. refrigerating) | MAKES: 16 servings.

▶ what you need!

1½ cups HONEY MAID Graham Cracker Crumbs

¼ cup (½ stick) butter or margarine, melted

2 pkg. (8 oz. each) PHILADELPHIA Cream Cheese, softened

½ cup sugar

½ tsp. vanilla

2 eggs

▶ make it!

HEAT oven to 350°F.

1. **MIX** crumbs and butter; press firmly onto bottom of 8- or 9-inch baking pan. Beat cream cheese, sugar and vanilla with electric mixer on medium speed until well blended. Add eggs; mix just until blended. Pour over crust.

2. **BAKE** 40 min. or until center is almost set. Cool.

3. **REFRIGERATE** 3 hours or overnight. Cut into 16 bars. Store leftover bars in refrigerator.

HOW TO EASILY REMOVE BARS FROM PAN:
Line pan with foil before pressing crumb mixture onto bottom of pan.

PHILADELPHIA 3-STEP CHEESECAKE:
Omit crumbs and butter. Prepare batter as directed; pour into 1 HONEY MAID Graham Pie Crust (6 oz.). Bake and cool as directed.

creamy strawberry cookie "tarts"

PREP: 15 min. plus refrigerating | MAKES: 12 servings.

▶ what you need!

⅔ cup boiling water

1 pkg. (3 oz.) JELL-O Strawberry Flavor Gelatin

1 pkg. (8 oz.) PHILADELPHIA Cream Cheese, cubed

1 cup thawed COOL WHIP Whipped Topping

12 CHIPS AHOY! Real Chocolate Chip Cookies

12 small fresh strawberries

▶ make it!

1. **STIR** boiling water into dry gelatin mix in small bowl at least 2 min. until completely dissolved. Cool 5 min., stirring occasionally.

2. **POUR** gelatin mixture into blender. Add cream cheese; cover. Blend on medium speed 30 to 45 sec. or until well blended; scrape down side of blender container, if needed. Add whipped topping; cover. Blend on low speed 5 sec. or just until blended.

3. **LINE** 12 muffin pan cups with paper liners; spray with cooking spray. Place 1 cookie on bottom of each prepared cup; top evenly with the gelatin mixture. Refrigerate 1 hour 30 min. or until firm. Top each with a strawberry just before serving. Store leftover desserts in refrigerator.

PHILADELPHIA
dessert dip

PREP: 5 min. | MAKES: 1¾ cups or 14 servings, 2 Tbsp. each.

▶ what you need!

1 pkg. (8 oz.) PHILADELPHIA Cream Cheese, softened

1 jar (7 oz.) JET-PUFFED Marshmallow Creme

▶ make it!

1. **MIX** ingredients until blended.

2. **SERVE** with assorted NABISCO Cookies or cut-up fresh fruit.

MAKE AHEAD:
Dip can be made ahead of time. Refrigerate until ready to serve.

SUBSTITUTE:
Prepare using PHILADELPHIA Neufchâtel Cheese.

MALLOW FRUIT DIP:
Prepare as directed, adding 1 Tbsp. orange juice, 1 tsp. orange zest and a dash of ground ginger.

HOW TO SOFTEN CREAM CHEESE:
Place completely unwrapped pkg. of cream cheese on microwaveable plate. Microwave on HIGH 10 to 15 sec. or until slightly softened.

MAKE IT EASY:
To easily remove marshmallow creme from jar, remove lid and seal. Microwave on HIGH 30 sec. before removing marshmallow creme from jar.

banana split cake

PREP: 15 min. plus refrigerating | MAKES: 24 servings.

▶ what you need!

9 HONEY MAID Honey Grahams, crushed (about 1½ cups)

1 cup sugar, divided

⅓ cup butter, melted

2 pkg. (8 oz. each) PHILADELPHIA Cream Cheese, softened

1 can (20 oz.) crushed pineapple, in juice, drained

6 bananas, divided

2 pkg. (3.4 oz. each) JELL-O Vanilla Flavor Instant Pudding

2 cups cold milk

2 cups thawed COOL WHIP Whipped Topping, divided

1 cup chopped PLANTERS Pecans

▶ make it!

1. **MIX** crumbs, ¼ cup sugar and butter; press onto bottom of 13×9-inch pan. Freeze 10 min.

2. **BEAT** cream cheese and remaining sugar with mixer until well blended. Spread carefully over crust; top with pineapple. Slice 4 bananas; arrange over pineapple.

3. **BEAT** pudding mixes and milk with whisk 2 min. Stir in 1 cup COOL WHIP; spread over banana layer in pan. Top with remaining COOL WHIP. Refrigerate 5 hours. Slice remaining 2 bananas just before serving; arrange over dessert. Top with nuts.

sugar cookie cutouts

PREP: 20 min. | TOTAL: 1 hr. 2 min. (incl. refrigerating) | MAKES: about 3½ doz. or 21 servings, 2 cookies each.

▶ what you need!

1 pkg. (8 oz.) PHILADELPHIA Cream Cheese, softened

¾ cup (1½ sticks) butter, softened

1 cup granulated sugar

2 tsp. vanilla

2¼ cups flour

½ tsp. baking soda

¼ cup colored sugar or festive sprinkles

▶ make it!

1. **BEAT** first 4 ingredients in large bowl with mixer until well blended. Add flour and baking soda; mix well. Refrigerate 30 min.

2. **HEAT** oven to 350°F. Roll dough to ⅛-inch thickness on lightly floured surface. Cut into assorted shapes, using 3-inch cookie cutters. Place, 2 inches apart, on greased baking sheets. Sprinkle with colored sugar.

3. **BAKE** 10 to 12 min. or until edges begin to brown. Cool on baking sheets 3 min.; transfer to wire racks. Cool completely.

CHOCO-ORANGE COOKIES:
Prepare dough as directed, adding 1 Tbsp. orange zest with the flour and baking soda. Shape into 2 (8-inch) logs; wrap in plastic wrap. Refrigerate 1 hour. Heat oven to 350°F. Unwrap logs; cut into ¼-inch-thick slices. Place on baking sheets. Bake 12 to 15 min. or until edges begin to brown. Cool on wire racks. Drizzle with 4 melted squares BAKER'S Semi-Sweet Chocolate; let stand until set. Makes 5 doz. or 30 servings, 2 cookies each.

SNOWMEN COOKIES:
Heat oven to 350°F. Prepare dough as directed; shape into equal number of
½-inch and 1-inch balls. (You should have about 44 of each size ball.) Using 1
small and 1 large ball for each snowman, place balls on baking sheet, with balls
touching each other. Flatten to ¼-inch thickness with bottom of glass dipped in
additional flour. Repeat with remaining dough. Bake 10 to 14 min. or until lightly
browned. Cool on wire racks. Decorate as desired. Makes about 3½ doz. or 22
servings, 2 cookies each.

PHILADELPHIA
marble brownies

PREP: 20 min. | TOTAL: 1 hr. | MAKES: 32 servings.

▶ what you need!

1 pkg. (19 to 21 oz.) brownie
mix (13×9-inch pan size)

1 pkg. (8 oz.) PHILADELPHIA
Cream Cheese, softened

⅓ cup sugar

1 egg

½ tsp. vanilla

½ cup BAKER'S Semi-Sweet
Chocolate Chunks

▶ make it!

HEAT oven to 350°F.

1. **PREPARE** brownie batter as directed on package; spread into greased
13×9-inch pan.

2. **BEAT** cream cheese with mixer until creamy. Add sugar, egg and vanilla;
mix well. Drop by tablespoonfuls over brownie batter; swirl with knife. Top
with chocolate chunks.

3. **BAKE** 35 to 40 min. or until cream cheese mixture is lightly browned. Cool
completely before cutting to serve. Keep refrigerated.

NOTE:
For best results, do not use brownie mix with a syrup pouch.

SUBSTITUTE:
Prepare using PHILADELPHIA Neufchâtel Cheese.

VARIATION:
Prepare as directed, omitting the chocolate chunks.

SPECIAL EXTRA:
After brownies have cooled, use a small round cookie cutter, about 1 inch in
diameter, to cut small, delicate petit-four-type brownies.

contents

Casseroles & Pasta

HEARTY DISHES YOUR FAMILY WILL LOVE

spaghetti a la PHILLY

PREP: 25 min. | TOTAL: 25 min. | MAKES: 6 servings.

▶ what you need!

¾ lb. spaghetti, uncooked

1 lb. lean ground beef

1 jar (24 oz.) spaghetti sauce

4 oz. (½ of 8-oz. pkg.) PHILADELPHIA Cream Cheese, cubed

2 Tbsp. KRAFT Grated Parmesan Cheese

▶ make it!

1. **COOK** spaghetti as directed on package.

2. **MEANWHILE,** brown meat in large skillet; drain. Return meat to skillet. Stir in sauce and cream cheese; cook on low heat 3 to 5 min. or until sauce is well blended and heated through, stirring frequently.

3. **DRAIN** spaghetti. Add to sauce; mix lightly. Place on platter; top with Parmesan.

SPECIAL EXTRA:
Garnish each serving with finely chopped fresh parsley.

SUBSTITUTE:
Prepare using ground turkey and PHILADELPHIA Neufchâtel Cheese.

creamy tomato and chicken spaghetti

PREP: 10 min. | TOTAL: 25 min. | MAKES: 4 servings, about 2 cups each.

▶ what you need!

½ lb. spaghetti, uncooked

2 cups frozen stir-fry vegetables

1 Tbsp. oil

1 lb. boneless skinless chicken breasts, cut into strips

1 can (14.5 oz.) diced tomatoes, undrained

¼ cup KRAFT Zesty Italian Dressing

½ cup (½ of 8-oz. tub) PHILADELPHIA Cream Cheese Spread

¼ cup KRAFT Grated Parmesan Cheese

▶ make it!

1. **COOK** spaghetti in large saucepan as directed on package, adding stir-fry vegetables to the boiling water the last 3 min.

2. **MEANWHILE,** heat oil in large nonstick skillet on medium-high heat. Add chicken; cook 6 min., stirring occasionally. Stir in tomatoes and dressing; bring to boil. Simmer on medium heat 4 min., stirring occasionally. Add cream cheese spread; cook and stir until cream cheese is completely melted and mixture is well blended.

3. **DRAIN** spaghetti mixture; place in large bowl. Add chicken mixture; toss to coat. Sprinkle with Parmesan.

SUBSTITUTE:
Substitute your favorite frozen vegetables for the stir-fry vegetables. Or, use cut-up fresh vegetables; just add to the cooking water for the last 4 min. of the spaghetti cooking time.

shrimp-in-love pasta

PREP: 10 min. | TOTAL: 25 min. | MAKES: 2 servings.

▶ what you need!

¼ lb. linguine, uncooked

1 cup uncooked deveined peeled medium shrimp

2 tomatoes, chopped

½ cup (½ of 8-oz. tub) PHILADELPHIA Cream Cheese Spread

1½ cups torn fresh spinach

▶ make it!

1. **COOK** linguine as directed on package.

2. **MEANWHILE,** heat large skillet on medium-high heat. Add shrimp, tomatoes and cream cheese spread; cook and stir 3 to 4 min. or until shrimp are done and mixture is well blended.

3. **DRAIN** linguine; place in large bowl. Add spinach; mix lightly. Stir in shrimp mixture.

SUBSTITUTE:
Prepare using 4 oz. (½ of 8-oz. pkg.) PHILADELPHIA ⅓ Less Fat than Cream Cheese.

TO DOUBLE:
For 4 servings, prepare as directed using 1 tub (8 oz.) PHILADELPHIA Cream Cheese Spread and doubling all other ingredients.

creamy pasta primavera

PREP: 15 min. | TOTAL: 30 min. | MAKES: 6 servings, 1⅓ cups each.

▶ what you need!

3 cups penne pasta, uncooked

2 Tbsp. KRAFT Light Zesty Italian Dressing

1½ lb. boneless skinless chicken breasts, cut into 1-inch pieces

2 zucchini, cut into bite-size pieces

1½ cups cut-up fresh asparagus (1-inch lengths)

1 red pepper, chopped

1 cup fat-free reduced-sodium chicken broth

4 oz. (½ of 8-oz. pkg.) PHILADELPHIA Neufchâtel Cheese, cubed

¼ cup KRAFT Grated Parmesan Cheese

▶ make it!

1. **COOK** penne in large saucepan as directed on package.

2. **MEANWHILE,** heat dressing in large skillet on medium heat. Add chicken and vegetables; cook 10 to 12 min. or until chicken is done, stirring frequently. Add broth and Neufchâtel; cook 1 min. or until Neufchâtel is melted, stirring constantly. Stir in Parmesan.

3. **DRAIN** penne; return to pan. Add chicken mixture; toss lightly. Cook 1 min. or until heated through. (Sauce will thicken upon standing.)

HOW TO MAKE IT MEATLESS:
Omit chicken. Prepare as directed, cooking vegetables until crisp-tender.

quick pasta carbonara

PREP: 20 min. | MAKES: 4 servings, 1¼ cups each.

▶ what you need!

½ lb. fettuccine, uncooked

4 slices OSCAR MAYER Bacon, chopped

4 oz. (½ of 8-oz. pkg.) PHILADELPHIA Cream Cheese, cubed

1 cup frozen peas

¾ cup milk

½ cup KRAFT Grated Parmesan Cheese

½ tsp. garlic powder

▶ make it!

1. **COOK** fettuccine as directed on package. Meanwhile, cook bacon in large skillet until crisp. Remove bacon from skillet with slotted spoon, reserving 2 Tbsp. drippings in skillet. Drain bacon on paper towels.

2. **ADD** remaining ingredients to reserved drippings; cook on low heat until cream cheese is melted and mixture is well blended and heated through.

3. **DRAIN** fettuccine; place in large bowl. Add cream cheese sauce and bacon; mix lightly.

KEEPING IT SAFE:
When a dish contains dairy products, such as the cheeses and milk in this recipe, be sure to serve it immediately and refrigerate any leftovers promptly.

SPECIAL EXTRA:
Top each serving with a light sprinkling of additional Parmesan Cheese.

SERVING SUGGESTION:
For added color and texture, serve with a mixed green salad tossed with your favorite KRAFT Light Dressing.

south-of-the-border chicken & pasta skillet

PREP: 10 min. | TOTAL: 35 min. | MAKES: 4 servings, 2 cups each.

▶ what you need!

2 cups rotini, uncooked

1 lb. boneless skinless chicken breasts, cut into bite-size pieces

1 jar (16 oz.) TACO BELL® HOME ORIGINALS® Thick 'N Chunky Salsa

1 pkg. (10 oz.) frozen corn

4 oz. (½ of 8-oz. pkg.) PHILADELPHIA Cream Cheese, cubed

¼ tsp. ground cumin

1 cup KRAFT Mexican Style Finely Shredded Four Cheese, divided

▶ make it!

1. **COOK** pasta as directed on package.

2. **MEANWHILE,** cook and stir chicken in large nonstick skillet sprayed with cooking spray on medium-high heat 6 min. or until done. Add salsa, corn, cream cheese and cumin; simmer on medium-low heat 6 min. or until cream cheese is melted, stirring occasionally.

3. **DRAIN** pasta; add to skillet with ½ cup shredded cheese. Stir; simmer 3 min. or until heated through. Top with remaining shredded cheese; cover. Remove from heat. Let stand until melted.

SPECIAL EXTRA:
Sprinkle with chopped cilantro before serving.

TACO BELL® and HOME ORIGINALS® are trademarks owned and licensed by Taco Bell Corp.

mexican chicken casserole

PREP: 20 min. | TOTAL: 45 min. | MAKES: 4 servings.

▶ what you need!

¾ lb. boneless skinless chicken breasts, cut into bite-size pieces

1 tsp. ground cumin

1 green pepper, chopped

1½ cups TACO BELL® HOME ORIGINALS® Thick 'N Chunky Salsa

2 oz. (¼ of 8-oz. pkg.) PHILADELPHIA Neufchâtel Cheese, cubed

1 can (15 oz.) no-salt-added black beans, rinsed

1 tomato, chopped

2 whole wheat tortillas (6 inch)

½ cup KRAFT Mexican Style 2% Milk Finely Shredded Four Cheese, divided

▶ make it!

HEAT oven to 375°F.

1. **COOK** and stir chicken and cumin in nonstick skillet sprayed with cooking spray on medium heat 2 min. Add peppers; cook 2 min., stirring occasionally. Stir in salsa; cook 2 min. Add Neufchâtel; cook 2 min. or until melted. Stir in beans and tomatoes.

2. **SPOON** ⅓ of the chicken mixture into 8-inch square baking dish; cover with 1 tortilla and half each of the remaining chicken mixture and shredded cheese. Top with remaining tortilla and chicken mixture; cover.

3. **BAKE** 20 min. or until heated through. Sprinkle with remaining shredded cheese; bake, uncovered, 5 min. or until melted.

SPECIAL EXTRA:
Sprinkle with ¼ cup chopped cilantro just before serving.

TACO BELL® and HOME ORIGINALS® are trademarks owned and licensed by Taco Bell Corp.

easy shepherd's pie

PREP: 10 min. | TOTAL: 30 min. | MAKES: 6 servings.

▶ what you need!

1 lb. ground beef

2 cups hot mashed potatoes

4 oz. (½ of 8-oz. pkg.) PHILADELPHIA Cream Cheese, cubed

1 cup KRAFT Shredded Cheddar Cheese, divided

2 cloves garlic, minced

4 cups frozen mixed vegetables, thawed

1 cup beef gravy

▶ make it!

HEAT oven to 375°F.

1. **BROWN** meat in large skillet; drain.

2. **MEANWHILE,** mix potatoes, cream cheese, ½ cup Cheddar and garlic until well blended.

3. **ADD** vegetables and gravy to meat; mix well. Spoon into 9-inch square baking dish.

4. **COVER** with potato mixture and remaining Cheddar. Bake 20 min. or until heated through.

BARBECUE SHEPHERD'S PIE:
Prepare omitting the garlic and substituting ¾ cup KRAFT Original Barbecue Sauce mixed with ½ tsp. onion powder for the gravy.

CREATIVE LEFTOVERS:
This recipe is a great way to use leftover mashed potatoes.

three-cheese chicken-penne pasta bake

PREP: 20 min. | TOTAL: 43 min. | MAKES: 4 servings.

▶ what you need!

1½ cups multi-grain penne pasta, uncooked

1 pkg. (9 oz.) fresh spinach leaves

1 lb. boneless skinless chicken breasts, cut into bite-size pieces

1 tsp. dried basil leaves

1 jar (14½ oz.) spaghetti sauce

1 can (14½ oz.) diced tomatoes, drained

2 oz. (¼ of 8-oz. pkg.) PHILADELPHIA Neufchâtel Cheese, cubed

1 cup KRAFT 2% Milk Shredded Mozzarella Cheese, divided

2 Tbsp. KRAFT Grated Parmesan Cheese

▶ make it!

HEAT oven to 375°F.

1. **COOK** pasta as directed on package, adding spinach to the boiling water during the last minute.

2. **COOK** and stir chicken and basil in large nonstick skillet sprayed with cooking spray on medium-high heat 3 min. Stir in spaghetti sauce and tomatoes; bring to boil. Simmer on low heat 3 min. or until chicken is done. Stir in Neufchâtel.

3. **DRAIN** pasta mixture; return to pan. Stir in chicken mixture and ½ cup mozzarella. Spoon into 2-qt. casserole or 8-inch square baking dish.

4. **BAKE** 20 min.; top with remaining cheeses. Bake 3 min. or until mozzarella is melted.

SERVING SUGGESTION:
Serve with CRYSTAL LIGHT Iced Tea.

creamy chicken pot pie

PREP: 10 min. | TOTAL: 40 min. | MAKES: 8 servings.

▶ what you need!

1 pkg. (8 oz.) PHILADELPHIA Cream Cheese, cubed

½ cup chicken broth

3 cups chopped cooked chicken

1 pkg. (16 oz.) frozen mixed vegetables, thawed

½ tsp. garlic salt

1 egg

½ cup milk

1 cup all-purpose baking mix

▶ make it!

HEAT oven to 400°F.

1. **COOK** cream cheese and broth in large saucepan on low heat until cream cheese is completely melted and mixture is well blended, stirring frequently with whisk. Stir in chicken, vegetables and garlic salt.

2. **SPOON** into 2-qt. casserole. Beat egg and milk in medium bowl with whisk until well blended; stir in baking mix just until moistened. Spoon over chicken mixture. Place casserole on baking sheet.

3. **BAKE** 25 to 30 min. or until golden brown.

SUBSTITUTE:
Prepare using PHILADELPHIA Neufchâtel Cheese.

SUBSTITUTE:
Substitute turkey for the chicken.

SERVING SUGGESTION:
For added color and texture, serve with a mixed green salad tossed with your favorite KRAFT Light Dressing.

Easy Entrées

MAIN MEALS THAT COME TOGETHER IN MINUTES

tandoori chicken kabobs

PREP: 10 min. | TOTAL: 50 min. (incl. marinating) | MAKES: 4 servings.

▸ what you need!

2 oz. (¼ of 8-oz. pkg.) PHILADELPHIA Cream Cheese, softened

2 Tbsp. tandoori paste

1 lb. boneless skinless chicken breasts, cut into 2-inch pieces

▸ make it!

1. **MIX** cream cheese and tandoori paste in medium bowl. Add chicken; toss to coat. Refrigerate 30 min. to marinate.

2. **HEAT** broiler. Remove chicken from marinade; reserve marinade. Thread chicken onto 4 skewers; brush with reserved marinade. Place on rack of broiler pan.

3. **BROIL,** 6 inches from heat source, 8 to 10 min. or until chicken is done, turning after 5 min.

NOTE:
If using wooden skewers, soak skewers in water 30 min. before using to prevent the skewers from burning on the grill.

SERVING SUGGESTION:
Serve over hot cooked basmati rice with a mixed green salad.

parmesan-crusted chicken in cream sauce

PREP: 15 min. | TOTAL: 30 min. | MAKES: 4 servings.

▸ what you need!

2 cups instant brown rice, uncooked

1 can (14 oz.) fat-free reduced-sodium chicken broth, divided

6 RITZ Crackers, finely crushed (about ½ cup)

2 Tbsp. KRAFT Grated Parmesan Cheese

4 small boneless skinless chicken breast halves (1 lb.)

2 tsp. oil

⅓ cup PHILADELPHIA Chive & Onion ⅓ Less Fat than Cream Cheese

¾ lb. asparagus spears, trimmed, steamed

▸ make it!

1. **COOK** rice as directed on package, using 1¼ cups of the broth and ½ cup water.

2. **MEANWHILE,** mix cracker crumbs and Parmesan on plate. Rinse chicken with cold water; gently shake off excess. Dip chicken in crumb mixture, turning to evenly coat both sides of each breast. Discard any remaining crumb mixture.

3. **HEAT** oil in large nonstick skillet on medium heat. Add chicken; cook 5 to 6 min. on each side or until done (165°F). Transfer to plate; cover to keep warm. Add remaining broth and reduced-fat cream cheese to skillet; bring just to boil, stirring constantly. Cook 3 min. or until thickened, stirring frequently; spoon over chicken. Serve with rice and asparagus.

VARIATION:
Prepare using plain PHILADELPHIA Neufchâtel Cheese and stirring in 1 Tbsp. chopped fresh chives along with the cream cheese.

chicken-parmesan bundles

PREP: 35 min. | TOTAL: 1 hr.. 5 min. | MAKES: 6 servings.

▶ what you need!

4 oz. (½ of 8-oz. pkg.) PHILADELPHIA Cream Cheese, softened

1 pkg. (10 oz.) frozen chopped spinach, thawed, well drained

1¼ cups KRAFT Shredded Low-Moisture Part-Skim Mozzarella Cheese, divided

6 Tbsp. KRAFT Grated Parmesan Cheese, divided

6 small boneless skinless chicken breast halves (1½ lb.), pounded to ¼-inch thickness

1 egg

10 RITZ Crackers, crushed (about ½ cup)

1½ cups spaghetti sauce, heated

▶ make it!

HEAT oven to 375°F.

1. **MIX** cream cheese, spinach, 1 cup mozzarella and 3 Tbsp. Parmesan until well blended; spread onto chicken breasts. Starting at 1 short end of each breast, roll up chicken tightly. Secure with wooden toothpicks, if desired.

2. **BEAT** egg in shallow dish. Mix remaining Parmesan and cracker crumbs in separate shallow dish. Dip chicken in egg, then roll in crumb mixture. Place, seam-sides down, in 13×9-inch baking dish sprayed with cooking spray.

3. **BAKE** 30 min. or until chicken is done (165°F). Remove and discard toothpicks, if using. Serve topped with spaghetti sauce and remaining mozzarella.

MAKE AHEAD:
Assemble chicken bundles and place in baking dish as directed. Refrigerate up to 4 hours. When ready to serve, uncover and bake at 375°F for 35 min. or until chicken is done.

chicken in creamy pan sauce

PREP: 10 min. | TOTAL: 30 min. | MAKES: 4 servings.

▶ what you need!

4 small boneless skinless chicken breast halves (1 lb.)

2 Tbsp. flour

1 Tbsp. oil

¾ cup fat-free reduced-sodium chicken broth

4 oz. (½ of 8-oz. pkg.) PHILADELPHIA Cream Cheese, cubed

1 Tbsp. chopped fresh parsley

▶ make it!

1. **COAT** chicken with flour. Heat oil in large skillet on medium heat. Add chicken; cook 5 to 6 min. on each side or until done (165°F). Remove chicken from skillet, reserving drippings in skillet. Cover chicken to keep warm.

2. **ADD** broth to skillet; stir to scrape up browned bits from bottom of skillet. Add cream cheese; cook 2 to 3 min. or until cream cheese is melted and sauce starts to thicken, stirring constantly with whisk.

3. **RETURN** chicken to skillet; turn over to coat both sides of chicken with sauce. Cook 2 min. or until chicken is heated through. Sprinkle with parsley.

VARIATION:
Prepare recipe as directed except omit parsley. Transfer chicken to serving platter; top with 1 cup quartered cherry tomatoes. Drizzle with sauce; sprinkle with fresh basil.

NOTE:
If possible, use a large skillet with sloping sides when preparing this recipe. Not only does this allow you to easily turn the chicken pieces but the larger surface area speeds up the evaporation of the cooking liquids which, in turn, allows the chicken to brown more quickly.

fiesta chicken enchiladas

PREP: 15 min. | TOTAL: 35 min. | MAKES: 4 servings.

▶ what you need!

1 small onion, chopped

1 clove garlic, minced

4 cooked small boneless skinless chicken breasts (1 lb.), shredded

1 cup TACO BELL® HOME ORIGINALS® Thick 'N Chunky Salsa, divided

4 oz. (½ of 8-oz. pkg.) PHILADELPHIA Cream Cheese, cubed

1 Tbsp. chopped cilantro

1 tsp. ground cumin

1 cup KRAFT Shredded Cheddar & Monterey Jack Cheese, divided

8 flour tortillas (6 inch)

▶ make it!

HEAT oven to 350°F.

1. **HEAT** large skillet spayed with cooking spray on medium heat. Add onions and garlic; cook and stir 2 min. Add chicken, ¼ cup salsa, cream cheese, cilantro and cumin; mix well. Cook until heated through, stirring occasionally. Add ½ cup shredded cheese; mix well.

2. **SPOON** about ⅓ cup chicken mixture down center of each tortilla; roll up. Place, seam-sides down, in 13×9-inch baking dish sprayed with cooking spray; top with remaining salsa and shredded cheese.

3. **BAKE** 15 to 20 min. or until heated through.

SHORTCUT:
Substitute 2 pkg. (6 oz. each) OSCAR MAYER Deli Fresh Oven Roasted Chicken Breast Cuts for the shredded cooked fresh chicken.

TACO BELL® and HOME ORIGINALS® are trademarks owned and licensed by Taco Bell Corp.

creamy rice, chicken & spinach dinner

PREP: 10 min. | TOTAL: 40 min. | MAKES: 4 servings, 1½ cups each.

▶ what you need!

¼ cup KRAFT Roasted Red Pepper Italian with Parmesan Dressing

1 lb. boneless skinless chicken breasts, cut into strips

1½ cups fat-free reduced-sodium chicken broth

2 cups instant brown rice, uncooked

4 oz. (½ of 8-oz. pkg.) PHILADELPHIA Neufchâtel Cheese, cubed

1 pkg. (8 oz.) baby spinach leaves

1 large tomato, chopped

2 Tbsp. KRAFT Grated Parmesan Cheese

▶ make it!

1. **HEAT** dressing in Dutch oven or large deep skillet on medium-high heat. Add chicken; cook 3 min. Stir in broth; bring to boil. Add rice; stir. Return to boil; cover. Simmer on medium heat 5 min.

2. **ADD** Neufchâtel; cook 2 to 3 min. or until melted, stirring frequently. Add spinach. (Pan will be full.) Cook, covered, 1 min. or until spinach is wilted. Stir gently to mix in spinach.

3. **REMOVE** pan from heat. Let stand, covered, 5 min. Stir in tomatoes; top with Parmesan.

SUBSTITUTE:
Prepare using KRAFT Light Zesty Italian Dressing.

farmhouse chicken dinner

PREP: 15 min. | TOTAL: 50 min. | MAKES: 4 servings.

▶ what you need!

¼ cup flour

½ tsp. black pepper

4 small bone-in chicken breast halves (1½ lb.), skin removed

¼ cup KRAFT Light Zesty Italian Dressing

2 cups baby carrots

1 onion, cut into wedges

1 can (14½ oz.) fat-free reduced-sodium chicken broth, divided

2 cups instant brown rice, uncooked

4 oz. (½ of 8-oz. pkg.) PHILADELPHIA Neufchâtel Cheese, cubed

2 Tbsp. chopped fresh parsley

▶ make it!

1. **MIX** flour and pepper in shallow dish. Add chicken; turn to coat both sides of each piece. Gently shake off excess flour. Heat dressing in large nonstick skillet on medium heat. Add chicken, meat-sides down; cook 5 to 6 min. or until golden brown. Turn chicken. Add carrots, onions and 1 cup broth; cover. Simmer on medium-low heat 20 min. or until chicken is done (165°F).

2. **MEANWHILE,** cook rice as directed on package; spoon onto platter. Use slotted spoon to remove chicken and vegetables from skillet; place over rice. Cover to keep warm.

3. **ADD** Neufchâtel and remaining broth to skillet; cook on high heat until Neufchâtel is melted and sauce is well blended, stirring constantly. Simmer on medium-low heat 3 to 5 min. or until slightly thickened, stirring occasionally. Spoon over chicken and vegetables; top with parsley.

SUBSTITUTE:
Substitute 8 bone-in chicken thighs with skin removed for the chicken breasts. Prepare as directed, cooking until chicken is done (165°F).

tuscan chicken simmer

PREP: 5 min. | TOTAL: 25 min. | MAKES: 4 servings.

▶ what you need!

4 small boneless skinless chicken breast halves (1 lb.)

4 oz. (½ of 8-oz. pkg.) PHILADELPHIA Cream Cheese, cubed

¼ cup water

¼ cup pesto

2 cups grape or cherry tomatoes

1 cup KRAFT Finely Shredded Italian* Five Cheese Blend

▶ make it!

1. **HEAT** large nonstick skillet sprayed with cooking spray on medium-high heat. Add chicken; cover. Cook 5 to 7 min. on each side or until done (165°F). Remove chicken from skillet; cover to keep warm.

2. **ADD** cream cheese, water, pesto and tomatoes to skillet. Cook, uncovered, on medium heat 2 min. or until cream cheese is melted and mixture is well blended, stirring occasionally.

3. **RETURN** chicken to skillet. Cook and stir 1 min. or until chicken is coated and heated through. Sprinkle with shredded cheese.

SERVING SUGGESTION:
Spoon over hot cooked spinach fettuccine or ravioli.

*Made with quality cheeses crafted in the USA.

creamy thai green curry chicken & rice

PREP: 15 min. | TOTAL: 30 min. | MAKES: 4 servings, 2 cups each.

▶ what you need!

1 Tbsp. canola oil

2 Tbsp. green curry paste

1 lb. boneless skinless chicken breasts, cut into bite-size pieces

1 small onion, thinly sliced

1 each red and green pepper, cut lengthwise into thin strips, then cut crosswise in half

4 oz. (½ of 8-oz. pkg.) PHILADELPHIA Cream Cheese, cubed

¼ cup milk

⅛ tsp. white pepper

4 cups hot cooked long-grain white rice

▶ make it!

1. **HEAT** oil in large nonstick skillet on medium heat. Stir in curry paste until well blended. Add chicken and onions; cook and stir 6 to 8 min. or until chicken is done. Stir in peppers; cook 4 to 5 min. or until crisp-tender.

2. **ADD** cream cheese, milk and white pepper; cook until cream cheese is melted and evenly coats chicken and vegetables, stirring frequently.

3. **SERVE** over rice.

SUBSTITUTE:
Prepare using red curry paste.

roast pork
tenderloin supper

PREP: 20 min. | TOTAL: 45 min. | MAKES: 6 servings.

▶ what you need!

2 pork tenderloins (1½ lb.)

¼ cup GREY POUPON Dijon Mustard

2 tsp. dried thyme leaves

1 pkg. (6 oz.) STOVE TOP Stuffing Mix for Chicken

½ cup fat-free reduced-sodium chicken broth

4 oz. (½ of 8-oz. pkg.) PHILADELPHIA Neufchâtel Cheese, cubed

1 lb. fresh green beans, trimmed, steamed

▶ make it!

HEAT oven to 400°F.

1. **HEAT** large nonstick skillet on medium heat. Add meat; cook 5 min. or until browned on all sides, turning occasionally. Remove meat from skillet, reserving meat drippings in skillet; place meat in 13×9-inch baking dish. Mix mustard and thyme; spread onto meat.

2. **BAKE** 20 to 25 min. or until meat is done (160°F). Transfer to carving board; tent with foil. Let stand 5 min. Meanwhile, prepare stuffing as directed on package, reducing the spread to 1 Tbsp.

3. **ADD** broth to same skillet. Bring to boil on high heat. Reduce heat to medium-low. Add Neufchâtel; cook 2 min. or until Neufchâtel is completely melted and mixture is well blended, stirring constantly.

4. **CUT** meat into thin slices. Serve topped with the Neufchâtel sauce along with the stuffing and beans.

NOTE:
If you purchased the broth in a 32-oz. pkg., store remaining broth in refrigerator up to 1 week. Or if you purchased a 14-oz. can, pour the remaining broth into a glass container; store in refrigerator up to 1 week.

curried pork and noodles

▶ what you need!

4 slices OSCAR MAYER Bacon, chopped

½ cup milk

4 oz. (½ of 8-oz. pkg.) PHILADELPHIA Cream Cheese, cubed

¾ cup BAKER'S ANGEL FLAKE Coconut

1 tsp. curry powder

½ tsp. ground red pepper (cayenne)

½ lb. spaghetti, uncooked

1½ lb. pork tenderloin, cut into bite-size pieces

1 red or green pepper, cut into strips

2 green onions, sliced

▶ make it!

1. **COOK** bacon in large skillet on medium-high heat 5 min. or until crisp; remove to paper towels to drain. Discard drippings. Blend milk, cream cheese, coconut and seasonings in blender until smooth. Cook spaghetti as directed on package.

2. **MEANWHILE,** cook half the tenderloin pieces in same skillet on medium-low heat 4 min. or until evenly browned, stirring frequently. Transfer to bowl; cover to keep warm. Repeat with remaining tenderloin pieces. Add peppers to skillet; cook and stir 3 min. Return tenderloin meat to skillet along with cream cheese mixture; cook on low heat 8 to 10 min. or until meat is done, stirring occasionally.

3. **DRAIN** spaghetti; place on platter. Top with meat mixture, bacon and onions.

SERVING SUGGESTION:
Serve with a refreshing cucumber salad to help tame the heat of the curried pork.

skillet beef picadillo with walnut sauce

PREP: 10 min. | TOTAL: 40 min. | MAKES: 6 servings.

▶ what you need!

2 Tbsp. KRAFT Zesty Italian Dressing

1 cup sliced onions

1 clove garlic, minced

1½ lb. lean ground beef

¾ lb. cooked new potatoes (about 7), cut into ½-inch cubes

4 poblano chiles, roasted, peeled, seeded and cut into strips

1 can (8 oz.) tomato sauce

½ cup milk

4 oz. (½ of 8-oz. pkg.) PHILADELPHIA Cream Cheese, softened

½ cup chopped PLANTERS Walnuts

▶ make it!

1. **HEAT** dressing in large skillet on medium heat. Add onions and garlic; cook 3 min. or until onions are tender, stirring occasionally. Stir in meat; cook 8 to 10 min. or until meat is browned, stirring occasionally.

2. **STIR** in potatoes, chiles and tomato sauce; cover. Simmer on medium-low heat 15 min.

3. **MEANWHILE,** blend remaining ingredients in blender until well blended. Serve spooned over meat mixture.

SERVING SUGGESTION:
Serve with a mixed green salad tossed with KRAFT Light Ranch Dressing.

20-minute skillet salmon

PREP: 10 min. | TOTAL: 20 min. | MAKES: 4 servings.

▶ what you need!

1 Tbsp. oil

4 salmon fillets (1 lb.)

1 cup fat-free milk

½ cup (½ of 8-oz. tub) PHILADELPHIA ⅓ Less Fat than Cream Cheese

½ cup chopped cucumbers

2 Tbsp. chopped fresh dill

▶ make it!

1. **HEAT** oil in large skillet on medium-high heat. Add fish; cook 5 min. on each side or until fish flakes easily with fork. Remove from skillet; cover to keep warm.

2. **ADD** milk and reduced-fat cream cheese to skillet; cook and stir until cream cheese is completely melted and mixture is well blended. Stir in cucumbers and dill.

3. **RETURN** fish to skillet. Cook 2 min. or until heated through. Serve topped with cream cheese sauce.

SERVING SUGGESTION:
Round out the meal with hot cooked rice and steamed vegetables. Or serve salmon on a bed of salad greens.

COOKING KNOW-HOW:
When salmon is done, it will appear opaque and flake easily with fork.

FOOD FACTS:
Check salmon fillets for bones before cooking by running fingers over surface. Small bumps are usually a sign of bones—use tweezers to remove them.

fish in roasted red pepper sauce

PREP: 10 min. | TOTAL: 30 min. | MAKES: 4 servings.

▶ what you need!

4 cod fillets (1 lb.)

¼ cup flour

¼ cup KRAFT Zesty Italian Dressing

½ cup sliced onions

2 oz. (¼ of 8-oz. pkg.) PHILADELPHIA Cream Cheese, softened

¼ cup roasted red peppers

¼ cup chicken broth

1 clove garlic, peeled

2 Tbsp. chopped cilantro

▶ make it!

1. **COAT** both sides of fish with flour; set aside. Heat dressing in large skillet on medium-high heat. Add onions; cook and stir until crisp-tender. Add fish; cook 5 to 7 min. on each side or until fish flakes easily with fork.

2. **MEANWHILE,** blend cream cheese, peppers, broth and garlic in blender until smooth. Spoon into medium saucepan. Bring to boil on medium-high heat; simmer on low heat 5 min., stirring occasionally.

3. **PLACE** fish on serving platter; top with onions and cream cheese mixture. Sprinkle with cilantro.

MAKE IT EASY:
Substitute jarred roasted red peppers for the roasted fresh red peppers.

BUYING AND STORING FROZEN FISH & SHELLFISH:
When purchasing frozen fish or shellfish, make sure it is well wrapped and solidly frozen, with no odor. Always check the "sell-by" date on the package. Avoid fish that has been thawed and refrozen. Store it in the refrigerator, tightly wrapped, for up to 2 days. Never refreeze fish or shellfish once it's been thawed.

stuffed fiesta burgers

PREP: 15 min. | TOTAL: 33 min. | MAKES: 4 servings.

▶ what you need!

1 lb. ground beef

1 pkg. (1¼ oz.) TACO BELL® HOME ORIGINALS® Taco Seasoning Mix

¼ cup PHILADELPHIA Chive & Onion Cream Cheese Spread

⅓ cup KRAFT Shredded Cheddar Cheese

4 hamburger buns, lightly toasted

½ cup TACO BELL® HOME ORIGINALS® Thick 'N Chunky Medium Salsa

1 avocado, cut into 8 slices

▶ make it!

HEAT grill to medium heat.

1. **MIX** meat and seasoning mix; shape into 8 thin patties. Mix cream cheese spread and Cheddar; spoon about 2 Tbsp. onto center of each of 4 patties. Top with remaining patties; pinch edges together to seal.

2. **GRILL** 7 to 9 min. on each side or until burgers are done (160°F).

3. **FILL** buns with burgers, salsa and avocados.

SUBSTITUTE:
Substitute thawed LOUIS RICH Pure Ground Turkey for the ground beef.

FUN IDEA:
With the wide variety of salsas now available, why not try topping these burgers with a roasted corn salsa, green salsa or even a fruit salsa?

TACO BELL® and HOME ORIGINALS® are trademarks owned and licensed by Taco Bell Corp.

wrapped veggie sandwich

PREP: 5 min. | MAKES: 1 serving.

▶ what you need!

2 flour tortillas (6 inch)

2 Tbsp. PHILADELPHIA Chive & Onion Cream Cheese Spread

1 KRAFT Singles, cut in half

1 cup fresh spinach leaves

½ cup chopped, drained roasted red peppers

¼ cup shredded carrots

▶ make it!

1. **SPREAD** tortillas with cream cheese spread.

2. **TOP** with remaining ingredients; roll up.

3. **SECURE** with toothpicks.

SUBSTITUTE:
Use PHILADELPHIA Chive & Onion ⅓ Less Fat than Cream Cheese.

cheesy chicken tostadas

PREP: 10 min. | TOTAL: 17 min. | MAKES: 6 servings.

▶ what you need!

6 tostada shells

½ cup (½ of 8-oz. tub) PHILADELPHIA Chive & Onion Cream Cheese Spread

¾ lb. cooked chicken, shredded

6 KRAFT Singles

1 avocado, sliced

1½ cups shredded lettuce

1 tomato, chopped

▶ make it!

HEAT oven to 375°F.

1. **PLACE** tostada shells on baking sheet; spread with cream cheese spread. Fill with chicken and Singles.

2. **BAKE** 5 to 7 min. or until heated through.

3. **TOP** with remaining ingredients.

SUBSTITUTE:
Substitute shredded cooked beef or pork for the chicken.

Delicious Sides

PERFECT ACCOMPANIMENTS TO ANY MEAL

creamy vegetable bake

PREP: 20 min. | TOTAL: 50 min. | MAKES: 10 servings, ¾ cup each.

▶ what you need!

1 pkg. (8 oz.) PHILADELPHIA Cream Cheese, softened

⅓ cup milk

¼ cup KRAFT Grated Parmesan Cheese

1 tsp. dried basil leaves

4 large carrots, diagonally sliced

½ lb. sugar snap peas

½ lb. fresh asparagus, cut into 1-inch lengths

1 large red pepper, chopped

1 pkg. (6 oz.) STOVE TOP Stuffing Mix for Chicken

▶ make it!

HEAT oven to 350°F.

1. **MICROWAVE** cream cheese and milk in large microwaveable bowl on HIGH 1 min. or until cream cheese is melted and mixture is blended when stirred. Add Parmesan and basil; stir until blended. Add vegetables; toss to coat.

2. **SPOON** into greased 13×9-inch baking dish. Prepare stuffing as directed on package; spoon over vegetable mixture.

3. **BAKE** 30 min. or until golden brown.

SUBSTITUTE:
Prepare using PHILADELPHIA Neufchâtel Cheese.

HOW TO SELECT SUGAR SNAP PEAS:
Sugar snap peas are a cross between the common English pea and snow peas. Both the pod and the peas inside are edible. Choose pods that are plump, crisp and bright green. Before using, snap off the stem ends, pulling to remove any strings.

new potatoes in dill cream sauce

PREP: 10 min. | TOTAL: 30 min. | MAKES: 16 servings, about ½ cup each.

▶ what you need!

2½ lb. new potatoes (about 20), quartered

1 tub (8 oz.) PHILADELPHIA Chive & Onion Cream Cheese Spread

¼ cup milk

1 green pepper, chopped

3 Tbsp. chopped fresh dill

▶ make it!

1. **COOK** potatoes in boiling water in saucepan on medium heat 15 min. or until potatoes are tender; drain.

2. **MEANWHILE,** microwave cream cheese spread, milk and peppers in large microwaveable bowl on HIGH 40 to 50 sec. or until cream cheese spread is melted when stirred. Stir in dill until well blended.

3. **ADD** potatoes; toss to coat.

SUBSTITUTE:
Substitute chopped fresh basil leaves or 2 tsp. dill weed for the chopped fresh dill.

CREATIVE LEFTOVERS:
Refrigerate any leftovers. Serve as a cold potato salad, stirring in a small amount of additional milk to thin, if necessary.

oat-topped
sweet potato crisp

PREP: 20 min. | TOTAL: 1 hr. | MAKES: 8 servings.

▶ what you need!

1 pkg. (8 oz.) PHILADELPHIA Cream Cheese, softened

1 can (40 oz.) cut sweet potatoes, drained

¾ cup packed brown sugar, divided

¼ tsp. ground cinnamon

1 Granny Smith apple, chopped

⅔ cup chopped cranberries

½ cup flour

½ cup old-fashioned or quick-cooking oats, uncooked

⅓ cup cold butter or margarine

¼ cup chopped PLANTERS Pecans

▶ make it!

HEAT oven to 350°F.

1. **BEAT** cream cheese, potatoes, ¼ cup sugar and cinnamon with mixer until well blended. Spoon into 1½-qt. casserole; top with apples and cranberries.

2. **MIX** flour, oats and remaining sugar in medium bowl; cut in butter until mixture resembles coarse crumbs. Stir in nuts. Sprinkle over fruit layer in casserole.

3. **BAKE** 35 to 40 min. or until heated through.

SUBSTITUTE:
Prepare using PHILADELPHIA Neufchâtel Cheese.

broccoli & cauliflower supreme

PREP: 10 min. | TOTAL: 30 min. | MAKES: 4 servings.

▶ what you need!

4 oz. (½ of 8-oz. pkg.) PHILADELPHIA Fat Free Cream Cheese, cubed

¼ cup KRAFT FREE Peppercorn Ranch Dressing

1 Tbsp. GREY POUPON Dijon Mustard

1½ bunches broccoli, cut into florets (about 6 cups), steamed, drained

½ head cauliflower, cut into florets (about 3 cups), steamed, drained

12 RITZ Reduced Fat Crackers, crushed (about ½ cup)

▶ make it!

1. **MICROWAVE** cream cheese, dressing and mustard in medium microwaveable bowl on HIGH 30 to 45 sec. or until cream cheese is softened and sauce is heated through. Stir until cream cheese is completely melted and sauce is well blended.

2. **COMBINE** vegetables in large bowl. Add sauce; toss until vegetables are evenly coated.

3. **TRANSFER** to serving bowl; top with cracker crumbs.

SUBSTITUTE:
Prepare using frozen broccoli and cauliflower florets.

creamy broccoli soup

PREP: 15 min. | TOTAL: 30 min. | MAKES: 6 servings, ¾ cup each.

▶ what you need!

¼ cup chopped onions

1 Tbsp. butter or margarine

1 Tbsp. flour

2 cups milk

4 oz. (½ of 8-oz. pkg.) PHILADELPHIA Cream Cheese, cubed

½ lb. (8 oz.) VELVEETA Pasteurized Prepared Cheese Product, cut into
  ½-inch cubes

1 pkg. (10 oz.) frozen chopped broccoli, cooked, drained

¼ tsp. ground nutmeg

⅛ tsp. black pepper

▶ make it!

1. **COOK** and stir onions in butter in 2-qt. saucepan on medium-high heat until onions are crisp-tender. Blend in flour.

2. **ADD** milk and cream cheese; cook on medium heat until cream cheese is melted, stirring frequently.

3. **STIR** in remaining ingredients; cook until heated through, stirring occasionally.

SUBSTITUTE:
Substitute frozen chopped spinach; frozen cauliflower florets, chopped; or frozen asparagus spears, chopped; for the broccoli.

USE YOUR MICROWAVE:
Microwave onions and butter in 2-qt. microwaveable bowl on HIGH 30 sec. or until onions are crisp-tender. Stir in flour and milk. Microwave 3 to 4 min. or until heated through, stirring every 2 min. Stir in cream cheese. Microwave 4 to 6 min. or until cream cheese is melted, stirring every 2 min. Stir in remaining ingredients. Microwave 30 sec. or until heated through.

crispy-topped creamy spinach

PREP: 10 min. | TOTAL: 35 min. | MAKES: 12 servings.

▶ what you need!

2 pkg. (10 oz. each) frozen chopped spinach, thawed, well drained

1 tub (8 oz.) PHILADELPHIA Chive & Onion Cream Cheese Spread

½ cup KRAFT Ranch Dressing

2 eggs, beaten

1½ cups KRAFT Shredded Cheddar Cheese, divided

24 RITZ Crackers, crushed (about 1 cup), divided

▶ make it!

HEAT oven to 375°F.

1. **MIX** first 4 ingredients in large bowl until well blended. Stir in ¾ cup Cheddar and ½ cup cracker crumbs.

2. **SPOON** into greased 2-qt. casserole; top with remaining Cheddar and crumbs.

3. **BAKE** 20 to 25 min. or until casserole is heated through and cheese is melted.

potato-leek soup

PREP: 20 min. | TOTAL: 1 hr. | MAKES: 8 servings, 1 cup each.

▶ what you need!

2 Tbsp. olive oil

4 large leeks (about 2 lb.), cut into ¼-inch-thick slices

4 large baking potatoes, peeled, cubed (about 4 cups)

1¼ qt. (5 cups) water

1 tsp. salt

½ tsp. black pepper

1 pkg. (8 oz.) PHILADELPHIA Cream Cheese, cubed

½ cup milk

¼ cup chopped fresh chives

▶ make it!

1. **HEAT** oil in Dutch oven on medium heat. Add leeks; cook 5 min. or until tender, stirring occasionally. Add potatoes, water, salt and pepper; cover. Bring to boil; simmer on medium-low heat 15 to 20 min. or until potatoes are tender. Cool 10 min.

2. **ADD** leek mixture, in batches, to blender; blend until puréed. Return to Dutch oven. Whisk in cream cheese, a few cubes at a time; cook on medium heat until cream cheese is completely melted, stirring constantly.

3. **ADD** milk; cook until heated through, stirring occasionally. Sprinkle with chives and additional pepper, if desired. Serve with PREMIUM Multigrain Saltine Crackers.

PREPARING LEEKS:
Leeks are grown in sandy soil and must be washed well before using. To prepare leeks, trim the roots and remove the dark green portions. Only the white portion of the leek is used. Chop or slice the white sections, then rinse in water to remove any soil or sand.

mashed potato layer bake

PREP: 40 min. | TOTAL: 1 hr. | MAKES: 14 servings, ½ cup each.

▶ what you need!

3¼ lb. baking potatoes (about 7), peeled, chopped and cooked

½ lb. sweet potatoes (about 3), peeled, chopped and cooked

1 tub (8 oz.) PHILADELPHIA Chive & Onion Cream Cheese Spread, divided

½ cup BREAKSTONE'S or KNUDSEN Sour Cream, divided

¼ tsp. each salt and black pepper

¼ cup KRAFT Shredded or Grated Parmesan Cheese, divided

¼ cup KRAFT Shredded Cheddar Cheese, divided

▶ make it!

HEAT oven to 375°F.

1. **PLACE** potatoes in separate bowls. Add half each of the cream cheese spread and sour cream to each bowl; season with salt and pepper. Mash until creamy.

2. **STIR** half the Parmesan into white potatoes. Stir half the Cheddar into sweet potatoes. Layer half each of the potatoes in 2-qt. clear glass casserole. Repeat layers.

3. **BAKE** 15 min. Top with remaining cheeses; bake 5 min. or until melted.

MAKE AHEAD:
Assemble casserole as directed, but do not add the cheese topping. Refrigerate casserole and cheese topping separately up to 3 days. When ready to serve, bake casserole (uncovered) as directed, increasing baking time as needed until casserole is heated through. Top with remaining cheeses and continue as directed.

twice-baked sweet potatoes

PREP: 10 min. | TOTAL: 53 min. | MAKES: 4 servings.

▶ what you need!

2 large sweet potatoes

2 oz. (¼ of 8-oz. pkg.) PHILADELPHIA Neufchâtel Cheese, cubed

2 Tbsp. fat-free milk

1 Tbsp. brown sugar

¼ tsp. ground cinnamon

¼ cup chopped PLANTERS Pecans

▶ make it!

HEAT oven to 425°F.

1. **CUT** potatoes lengthwise in half; place, cut-sides down, in foil-lined 15×10×1-inch pan. Bake 30 to 35 min. or until tender.

2. **SCOOP** out centers of potatoes into bowl, leaving ¼-inch-thick shells. Add Neufchâtel, milk, sugar and cinnamon to potatoes; mash until blended.

3. **FILL** shells with potato mixture; top with nuts. Bake 8 min. or until potatoes are heated through and nuts are toasted.

SHORTCUT:
Pierce whole sweet potatoes with fork; wrap in damp paper towels. Microwave on HIGH 7 to 8 min. or until tender. Cut potatoes in half; scoop out centers and continue as directed.

MAKE AHEAD:
Stuff potato shells as directed; refrigerate up to 1 hour. When ready to serve, bake as directed, increasing baking time as needed until filling is heated through.

crust-topped broccoli-cheese bake

PREP: 10 min. | TOTAL: 40 min. | MAKES: 14 servings.

▶ what you need!

½ cup (½ of 8-oz. tub) PHILADELPHIA Chive & Onion Cream Cheese Spread

1 can (10¾ oz.) condensed cream of mushroom soup

½ cup water

2 pkg. (16 oz. each) frozen broccoli florets, thawed, drained

1 cup KRAFT Shredded Cheddar Cheese

1 thawed frozen puff pastry sheet (½ of 17.3-oz. pkg.)

1 egg, beaten

▶ make it!

HEAT oven to 400°F.

1. **MIX** cream cheese spread, soup and water in large bowl until well blended. Stir in broccoli and Cheddar. Spoon into 2½- to 3-qt. shallow rectangular or oval baking dish.

2. **ROLL** pastry sheet on lightly floured surface to fit top of baking dish. Cover dish completely with pastry. Press pastry edges against rim of dish to seal. Brush with egg; pierce with knife to vent.

3. **BAKE** 30 min. or until filling is heated through and pastry is puffed and golden brown.

MAKE AHEAD:
Casserole can be assembled in advance. Refrigerate up to 24 hours. When ready to serve, bake (uncovered) as directed.

VARIATION:
Prepare as directed, using PHILADELPHIA Chive & Onion ⅓ Less Fat than Cream Cheese and KRAFT 2% Milk Shredded Cheddar Cheese.

corn souffle

PREP: 15 min. | TOTAL: 55 min. | MAKES: 16 servings.

▶ what you need!

2 Tbsp. butter

1 pkg. (8 oz.) PHILADELPHIA Cream Cheese, cubed

1 can (15¼ oz.) whole kernel corn, drained

1 can (14.75 oz.) cream-style corn

1 pkg. (8.5 oz.) corn muffin mix

2 eggs, beaten

1 cup KRAFT Shredded Cheddar Cheese

▶ make it!

HEAT oven to 350°F.

1. **MICROWAVE** butter in medium microwaveable bowl on HIGH 30 sec. or until melted. Stir in cream cheese. Microwave 15 sec. or until cream cheese is softened; stir until cream cheese is completely melted and mixture is well blended. Add next 4 ingredients; mix well.

2. **POUR** into 13×9-inch pan sprayed with cooking spray; top with Cheddar.

3. **BAKE** 40 min. or until golden brown. Cool slightly.

SERVING SUGGESTION:
This dish is versatile enough to pair with your favorite barbecued meat, beef stew, chicken soup or even chili.

SUBSTITUTE:
Prepare using PHILADELPHIA Neufchâtel Cheese.

SPECIAL EXTRA:
Add 2 sliced green onions along with the corns, muffin mix and eggs.

MEXICAN-STYLE CORN SOUFFLE:
Prepare as directed, substituting 1 can (11 oz.) whole kernel corn with chopped red and green peppers for the plain whole kernel corn.

easy cheesy scalloped potatoes

PREP: 30 min. | TOTAL: 1 hr. | MAKES: 15 servings, ¾ cup each.

▶ what you need!

1 pkg. (8 oz.) PHILADELPHIA Cream Cheese, softened

½ cup BREAKSTONE'S or KNUDSEN Sour Cream

1 cup chicken broth

3 lb. red potatoes (about 9), thinly sliced

1 pkg. (6 oz.) OSCAR MAYER Smoked Ham, chopped

1 pkg. (8 oz.) KRAFT Shredded Cheddar Cheese, divided

1 cup frozen peas

▶ make it!

HEAT oven to 350°F.

1. **MIX** cream cheese, sour cream and broth in large bowl until well blended. Add potatoes, ham, 1¾ cups Cheddar and peas; stir gently to evenly coat all ingredients.

2. **SPOON** into 13×9-inch baking dish sprayed with cooking spray; top with remaining Cheddar.

3. **BAKE** 1 hour or until casserole is heated through and potatoes are tender.

SERVING SUGGESTION:
Balance this creamy, indulgent side dish by serving it alongside cooked lean meat or fish and a steamed green vegetable.

PURCHASING POTATOES:
Look for firm, smooth, well-shaped potatoes that are free of wrinkles, cracks and blemishes. Avoid any with green-tinged skins or sprouting "eyes" or buds.

VARIATION:
Substitute OSCAR MAYER Smoked Turkey for the ham and/or 1 cup frozen mixed vegetables for the peas.

cheesy rice & corn casserole

PREP: 10 min. | TOTAL: 35 min. | MAKES: 8 servings, ½ cup each.

▶ what you need!

½ cup (½ of 8-oz. tub) PHILADELPHIA Chive & Onion Cream Cheese Spread

1 egg

2 cups cooked instant white rice

1 can (15¼ oz.) corn with red and green peppers, drained

1 cup KRAFT Mexican Style Finely Shredded Four Cheese, divided

2 Tbsp. chopped fresh cilantro

▶ make it!

HEAT oven to 375°F.

1. **MIX** cream cheese spread and egg in large bowl until well blended. Stir in rice, corn, ¾ cup shredded cheese and cilantro.

2. **POUR** into greased 1½-qt. casserole; top with remaining shredded cheese.

3. **BAKE** 20 to 25 min. or until is casserole is heated through and cheese is melted.

SPECIAL EXTRA:
Add 1 to 2 tsp. ground cumin for more Mexican flavor.

easy risotto with bacon & peas

PREP: 10 min. | TOTAL: 40 min. | MAKES: 6 servings, 1 cup each.

▶ what you need!

6 slices OSCAR MAYER Bacon, cut into 1-inch pieces

1 onion, chopped

1½ cups medium-grain rice, uncooked

2 cloves garlic, minced

3 cans (15 oz. each) chicken broth

4 oz. (½ of 8-oz. pkg.) PHILADELPHIA Cream Cheese, cubed

1 cup frozen peas, thawed

2 Tbsp. chopped fresh parsley

2 Tbsp. KRAFT Grated Parmesan Cheese, divided

▶ make it!

1. **COOK** bacon and onions in large skillet on medium-high heat 5 min. or just until bacon is crisp, stirring occasionally.

2. **ADD** rice and garlic; cook 3 min. or until rice is opaque, stirring frequently. Gradually add ½ can broth; cook and stir 3 min. or until broth is completely absorbed. Repeat with remaining broth, adding the cream cheese with the last addition of broth and cooking 5 min. or until the cream cheese is completely melted and mixture is well blended.

3. **STIR** in peas; cook 2 min. or until peas are heated through, stirring occasionally. Remove from heat. Stir in parsley and 1 Tbsp. Parmesan. Serve topped with remaining Parmesan.

SUBSTITUTE:
Prepare using fat-free reduced-sodium chicken broth.

SERVING SUGGESTION:
Serve with hot crusty bread and a mixed green salad topped with your favorite KRAFT Dressing.

zucchini with parmesan sauce

PREP: 10 min. | TOTAL: 17 min. | MAKES: 8 servings.

▶ what you need!

3 zucchini (1 lb.), cut diagonally into ½-inch-thick slices

2 yellow squash, cut diagonally into ½-inch-thick slices

1 red onion, cut into wedges

1 Tbsp. oil

1 tub (8 oz.) PHILADELPHIA Chive & Onion Cream Cheese Spread

⅓ cup fat-free milk

¼ cup KRAFT Grated Parmesan Cheese

¼ tsp. herb and spice blend seasoning

▶ make it!

1. **COOK** and stir vegetables in hot oil in large skillet 5 to 7 min. or until crisp-tender.

2. **MEANWHILE,** place remaining ingredients in small saucepan; cook on low heat until cream cheese spread is completely melted and mixture is well blended and heated through, stirring occasionally.

3. **SERVE** sauce over vegetables.

creamy veggies

PREP: 5 min. | TOTAL: 18 min. | MAKES: 5 servings.

▶ what you need!

1 pkg. (16 oz.) frozen mixed vegetables (California mix)

¼ lb. (4 oz.) VELVEETA 2% Milk Pasteurized Prepared Cheese Product, cut into ½-inch cubes

4 oz. (½ of 8-oz. pkg.) PHILADELPHIA Fat Free Cream Cheese, cubed

▶ make it!

1. **LAYER** ingredients in 1½-qt. microwaveable dish; cover with waxed paper.

2. **MICROWAVE** on HIGH 13 min. or until heated through, turning dish after 7 min.

3. **STIR** until well blended.

USE YOUR OVEN:
Layer ingredients in 1½-qt. casserole. Bake at 350°F for 55 min. or until heated through. Stir until well blended.

garlic mashed potatoes

PREP: 10 min. | TOTAL: 30 min. | MAKES: 8 servings, about ½ cup each.

▶ what you need!

2½ lb. potatoes (about 7), peeled, quartered

4 cloves garlic, minced

1 tub (8 oz.) PHILADELPHIA Cream Cheese Spread

1 Tbsp. butter or margarine

1 tsp. salt

▶ make it!

1. **COOK** potatoes and garlic in boiling water in large saucepan 20 min. or until potatoes are tender; drain.

2. **MASH** potatoes until smooth.

3. **STIR** in remaining ingredients until well blended.

SERVING SUGGESTION:
Add contrast to the potatoes by serving them with a crisp mixed green salad or vegetable, and lean fish, meat or poultry.

FOOD FACTS:
For best results, use russet or red potatoes since they work best for mashing.

SUBSTITUTE:
Prepare using PHILADELPHIA Chive & Onion Cream Cheese Spread.

MAKE IT EASY:
Use mixer to beat potatoes instead of using a hand masher.

INDEX

CHOCOLATE